Michael Lionstar

ROBERT GOTTLIEB was editor in chief of Simon and Schuster; president, publisher, and editor in chief of Alfred A. Knopf; and the editor of *The New Yorker*. Over the past two decades, he has written for *The New York Review of Books*, *The New York Times Book Review*, *The New Yorker*, and *The New York Observer*, for which he is the dance critic; published *Lives and Letters*, a collection of criticism; edited three anthologies— *Reading Jazz*, *Reading Dance*, and, with Robert Kimball, *Reading Lyrics;* and written biographies of George Balanchine and Sarah Bernhardt.

ALSO BY ROBERT GOTTLIEB

Lives and Letters

Sarah: The Life of Sarah Bernhardt

George Balanchine: The Ballet Maker

Reading Dance (editor)

Reading Lyrics (editor, with Robert Kimball)

Reading Jazz (editor)

Everyman's Library *Collected Stories*
of Rudyard Kipling (editor)

The Journals of John Cheever (editor)

A Certain Style: The Art of the Plastic Handbag, 1949–59

GREAT EXPECTATIONS

GREAT EXPECTATIONS

THE

SONS AND DAUGHTERS

OF

CHARLES DICKENS

ROBERT GOTTLIEB

PICADOR

FARRAR, STRAUS AND GIROUX

NEW YORK

www.picadorusa.com
www.twitter.com/picadorusa • www.facebook.com/picadorusa
picadorbookroom.tumblr.com

Picador® is a U.S. registered trademark and is used by Farrar, Straus and Giroux under license from Pan Books Limited.

For book club information, please visit www.facebook.com/picadorbookclub or e-mail marketing@picadorusa.com.

Frontispiece: Dickens reading to Katey and Mamie in the garden at Gad's Hill
Title page hand-lettering by Lindsey Mayer-Beug
Designed by Abby Kagan

The Library of Congress has cataloged the Farrar, Straus and Giroux edition as follows:

Gottlieb, Robert, 1931–
    Great expectations : the sons and daughters of Charles Dickens / Robert
Gottlieb. — 1st ed.
        p.   cm.
    ISBN 978-0-374-29880-7
    1. Dickens, Charles, 1812–1870—Family.   1. Title.
PR4582.G88 2012
823'.8—dc23

                                                                2012004997

Picador ISBN 978-1-250-03946-0

Picador books may be purchased for educational, business, or promotional use. For information on bulk purchases, please contact Macmillan Corporate and Premium Sales Department at 1-800-221-7945, extension 5442, or write specialmarkets@macmillan.com.

First published in the United States by Farrar, Straus and Giroux

First Picador Edition: December 2013

10 9 8 7 6 5 4 3 2 1

For my parents, Charles and Martha Gottlieb,

fanatical readers, whose marriage in some ways seems to me

to reflect the Dickens marital dynamic. Perhaps my

sympathy for the children of Charles Dickens stems from this

identification, while being a father allows me to

sympathize to a certain extent with his frustrations.

Although my children, of course, are perfect.

CONTENTS

CONTENTS

GREAT EXPECTATIONS

THE DICKENSES

WHEN CHARLES DICKENS and Catherine Hogarth were married on April 2, 1836, he was twenty-four and she was almost twenty-one. He had recovered from his tortured infatuation with the flirtatious Maria Beadnell and was well on his way to establishing himself as a clever and an admired young writer.

Charles had endured a difficult childhood: When he was eleven, his father, a well-meaning but improvident clerk in the navy pay office, was sent to debtors' prison, with young Charles put to menial work in a blacking factory—a social disgrace that demoralized him and from which he never fully recovered, keeping it a secret from the world (even from his children) until his death. The fact that, beginning in his mid-teens, he swiftly made his way as a law clerk, a parliamentary shorthand reporter, and an instant success as a writer of comic sketches, the very popular *Sketches by Boz*, is testament not only to his immense innate talent and overwhelming ambitions but to his prodigious and unrelenting energy and drive. Nothing could have stopped him.

Class was, as always in England, a matter of consuming concern. (Throughout his life, the question would arise as to

Dickens painted by Daniel Maclise, 1839

whether Dickens was, at bottom, actually . . . a gentleman.)
Catherine's family, the Hogarths, were steps up the social
ladder from the Dickenses. Her father, who had moved south
from Edinburgh, where he had been part of the Walter Scott
circle, was now a respected London journalist—a music critic
and the editor of the *Evening Chronicle*, for which Charles
was actively writing. The family was cultured, cultivated, and
relatively affluent; Catherine, the eldest of the nine Hogarth
children, was well-bred, well-read, and charming. And
pretty. She and Charles quickly made a match of it.

Charles would later maintain that it was never really a *love* match, but it was certainly a close and affectionate one, as is demonstrated in Dickens's devoted early letters to her. And a highly sexual one. Charley Dickens was born just nine months after the wedding, and the rate at which the other children followed (as well as at least two miscarriages), plus the references in letters to his friends to his impatience for the prescribed weeks to elapse following each birth before he could reclaim his marital rights, make it clear that his sexual needs were urgent. It seems likely that after his separation

Catherine Dickens painted by Daniel Maclise, 1839

from Catherine, as well as before his marriage, he had re-course to prostitutes (in an 1840 letter he wrote that prosti-tutes were "willing and consenting parties," and exclaimed "Good God if such sins were to be visited upon all of us and to hunt us down through life, what man would escape!"); in his later years he was treated at least once for a venereal con-dition. Certainly he was not a prude. If his own son were particularly chaste, he told Ralph Waldo Emerson, who quoted him in his journals for 1848, "I should be alarmed." (That must have been an interesting conversation.) Since at the time, however, his oldest son, Charley, was only eleven, it was not a pressing problem.

It is also indicative that in the later years of his marriage—that is, through the 1850s—Dickens grew more intimate with his new and younger friend and collaborator, Wilkie Collins, whose triumphant novels *The Woman in White* and *The Moonstone* appeared in Dickens's magazine *All the Year Round*, and with whom he both tramped through the night-time streets of London and traveled abroad. Collins's domestic life was highly irregular—he kept two concurrent semi-marital yet unacknowleged establishments—as opposed to that of Dickens's greatest friend and future biographer, John Forster, whom he trusted totally but who was hardly a rol-licking companion.

As Catherine grew stouter and more exhausted—those dozen or so pregnancies in fifteen years, plus severe post-partum depressions—and to his mind duller, his flirtations with and attentions to other women grew more active, though they were never of a scandalous nature (except to his wife, who not surprisingly was jealous).

She did not, however, appear to be jealous of the young

woman he adored above all others—her own younger sister Mary, who had begun living with the Dickenses soon after their marriage. In January 1837 Charley was born, with Mary on hand, and when two months later the family moved into their new home on Doughty Street in Bloomsbury (now the Dickens Museum), Mary was permanently with them, helping with the baby and the housekeeping. She was seventeen. One night that May, after returning from the theater with her sister and brother-in-law, she was struck by a fatal heart

Mary Hogarth

attack and died in Charles's arms the following day. His grief was violent, even unnatural. For the only time in his career he was unable to write, breaking off his work on *Pickwick Papers* and *Oliver Twist*, both of which were appearing serially. He insisted that when he died he must be buried with her, and wore her ring for the rest of his life, dreaming of her and turning her into an eternal symbol of purity and perfection. "God numbered her among His angels" was the epitaph he composed for her tombstone. And he re-embodied her in all the virginal girls—daughters, sisters, persecuted orphans—of his fiction, beginning with Rose Maylie, the insipid heroine of *Oliver Twist*. Soon, Mary was replaced in the Dickens household by Catherine's next sister, Georgina, who in time would become the mainstay of the family.

Catherine represented all the messy business of life—sex, childbirth, ill health. Mary was the holy symbol of maidenhood, now beyond reach: the angel. Georgina was the devoted mother/sister. In 1857 he met Ellen Ternan, who combined the sexual with the ideal—just eighteen (the age of his daughter Kate), a pretty, clever, though not very talented actress with whom he fell desperately and permanently in love. He was forty-five, tired of his wife, feeling the first signs of age. (Dickens had been boyish as a young man, and was preternaturally aged for a mature one. His massive workload—as writer, editor, public speaker, reformer—was already undermining his health.) He was determined to make Ellen his, and he succeeded.

There has been highly charged debate over whether—or, more realistically, when—she became his mistress, but almost at once she gave up the stage and from then on he was her protector and provider. But all in secret. By 1858 he had made up his mind to change his life and ruthlessly expelled Catherine from it, packing her off to her own establishment (with a generous settlement) and removing her children from her—except for Charley, now twenty-one and his own man. Only a few close friends knew of Ellen's existence in his life, and so it was to remain until his death twelve years later. The scandal over the break-up of the Dickens marriage, however, was highly public—he *made* it public, in his fraught attempts to justify his odious behavior to his wife: Not only was she an unloving mother, but her children didn't love *her*—the cruelest of his slanders, and completely unmerited.

This was the distressing family dynamic within which the younger children grew up under his and Georgina's superin-

Ellen Ternan

tendence in their house in Kent, Gad's Hill Place, near the cathedral city of Rochester. It was a house he knew from his childhood which he had purchased the year he met Ellen, and it was there that he wrote his final four novels—*A Tale of Two Cities*, *Great Expectations*, *Our Mutual Friend*, and the

Portrait of Charles Dickens by Samuel Laurence

unfinished *The Mystery of Edwin Drood*, which was set in Rochester. And it is where he died of a sudden stroke in June 1870, Georgina and the three oldest children in attendance, with another of the children, Henry, and Ellen—Georgina had sent for her when Dickens collapsed into his coma—arriving hours later. In the following century a theory was put forward that he had actually been taken ill that June night in Ellen's house and was spirited to Gad's Hill to avoid scandal, but this seems unlikely. Besides, the story as we know it is peculiar enough—the sister-in-law, the chil-

II

Portrait of Catherine Dickens by Samuel Laurence

dren, and the mistress gathered at the death bed—without requiring further embellishment. As for the other children, they were all abroad by now, living their various exiles. Catherine, the actual widow, was alone in her London home. She would outlive Charles by nine years.

"WHY WAS I EVER A FATHER!"

S o WROTE CHARLES DICKENS to a friend in 1868, less than
two years before his death. Yet in the beginning he was a
rapturously happy one. Babies and toddlers always gave him
joy. In the early years of his marriage, when the babies were
coming thick and fast, he could hardly bear being separated
from them. When he was away from home, he was forever
demanding news of them. To Catherine, when Charley was
not yet one: "A thousand loves and kisses to the darling boy
whom I see in my mind's eye crawling about the floor of this
Yorkshire inn . . . Bless his heart, I would give two sovereigns
for a kiss." He bombarded friends with news of their arrivals,
their christenings, their charms, their accomplishments. (In
an 1845 letter to a friend: "You shall see Mamie [seven] and
Charley [eight] dance the polka, when we return—which
you will really consider a very brilliant performance. Master
Frank is a prodigious blade, and more full of queer tricks
than any of his predecessors have been.")

When in 1842 he and Catherine made their six-month
American tour, he missed the children as much as she did,
and yearned to be back in London with them, literally count-
ing the days before they could sail. "God bless them," he

The four oldest Dickens children: Charley,
Mamie, Katey, and Walter

wrote to John Forster. "You can't imagine . . . how much I long to see them. It makes me quite sorrowful to think of them." (At least the Dickenses had some comfort from the portrait he had commissioned of the four little ones: It went with them everywhere.) And the children adored their parents as well. As the Dickens's carriage drew up to their house in London on their return from America, Charley, now five, fell into violent convulsions, explaining afterward to his mother that he was "too glad."

"Nothing could exceed Dickens's delight in his children

or their delight in him," wrote Edgar Johnson in his magis-
terial biography of 1952. "When he felt like defying his after-
breakfast schedule of work, they played long riotous games of
trap-bat and ball in the garden. And before they went to bed
Dickens would sit rocking in the American rocking chair
singing comic songs to a giggling childish audience: 'The
Loving Ballad of Lord Bateman' and one about 'Guy Fawkes,
that prince of sinisters, who once blew up the House of Lords,
the King, and all his ministers,' followed by a chorus of
'Oh, ah, oh, ri fol de riddy oddy bow wow wow,' delivered
with great expression as the singer rocked with one child on
his knee and the others clustered round."

But these were early days, with Dickens himself flushed
with youthful high spirits. The first four children had been
born before he turned thirty, at a time when the explosive
and unparalleled success of *Pickwick*, his early contentment
in his marriage, and the new-found comforts and pleasures
of his domestic life had made him as happy and satisfied a
man as he was ever to be.

As birth followed birth, a somewhat sardonic tone begins
to color his remarks to his correspondents about Catherine's
fecundity:

"Eight children, at this present writing. It begins to look
serious, I am afraid." "So you want a godchild. May I never
have the opportunity of giving you one! But if I have—if my
cup (I mean my quiver) be not yet full—then shall you hear
again from the undersigned Camel that his back is broken
by the addition of the last over-balancing straw." In 1860,
reporting at length on the entire family to a friend, he concludes, "I have also considered whether there are any more
children, and I don't think there are. If I should remember

two or three others presently, I will mention them in a postscript." It's all in his most symptomatic humorous vein, but
the humor is loaded.

Yes, ten children and at least two miscarriages within fifteen years might seem excessive to any father (and certainly
to any mother—Catherine suffered severe physical and psy-
chological damage from her constant pregnancies), but Charles
managed to ignore his own involvement in these pregnancies: It's always she who's responsible—his sexual require-
ments seemed to have nothing to do with it; you would think
he was a father only because she made him into one. Fred
Kaplan, in his *Dickens*, remarks, "Competent in his business
and social affairs, he was noticeably incompetent in managing his sexual life, perhaps because of some conflict, perhaps
because of a failure of the imagination."

Catherine is also held responsible by him for what he perceived to be the chief failings of the children. Her weaknesses, as he perceived them—her lethargy, her indolence,
her lack of purpose—explain the deficiencies he found in at
least six of their seven sons. (He did, it has to be said, ascribe
the boys' financial irresponsibility, their constantly falling
into debt, to his own side of the family—the Micawber
strain.) How could it not be *her* fault that *his* children lacked
his overwhelming energy; how could they not be attacking
life with his own implacable determination—how could they
not be eager to "hew out their own paths through the world
by sheer hard work"?

The fact that he had had to struggle so desperately to
escape the poverty and humiliation of his distressing childhood, whereas his sons had been raised in comfort and ease,
was irrelevant: They, too, must struggle to make their way—

must go out, early, into the world and carve lives for themselves; must pull themselves up by their own bootstraps, even
though their bootstraps were *born* up. Rigor, work, independence were the only acceptable routes to a responsible life.

As time passed, his dissatisfaction with his sons was frequently and forcefully expressed. "You don't know what it is
to look round the table and see reflected from every seat at it
(where they sit) some horribly well remembered expression of
inadaptability to anything." He referred to himself as "having
brought up the largest family ever known with the smallest
disposition to do anything for themselves." And, most conclusively, "I never sing their praises because they have so
often disappointed me."

Unfortunately, the Dickens boys were on the whole ordinary—or perhaps merely normal. Charley, after a weak start,
managed to construct a respectable and gratifying life for himself, but only the second-to-youngest of them, Henry, had any
large success. The others were generally good-natured, affectionate, in some cases sensitive; they had plenty of energy for
games, for pranks, even at times for work, and, loving and
respecting their father, they always hoped to please him—to
win the approval that was almost inevitably withheld. But
they lacked not only his genius but his compulsion to work,
no matter how hard he tried to implant it in them. And,
given his highly public view of their capacities, they lacked
self-confidence. When his friend the French actor Charles
Fechter remarked to Henry Wadsworth Longfellow that all
of Dickens's success went for nothing because he was unhappy
in his family, Annie Fields—the wife of his American publisher, and herself close to Dickens—wondered "how much
too much of this the children have had to hear." Their eternal

"failures" were to a certain extent a series of self-fulfilling prophecies.

In today's world, a son of so established and affluent a man as Dickens would automatically go to college and so would have until his early twenties to begin to find his path. But mid-nineteenth-century England was not like that—university was the exception, far from the rule—and since the boys had no particular academic aptitudes, university was not an option for them except for the eighth-born Henry, and he had to plead to go to Cambridge to study law rather than be sent abroad like five of his brothers.

The possibilities for well-born young men were business, for which none of the Dickens sons proved to have exceptional talent; the church, in which they had no interest; the army or navy; and emigration—the route Dickens preferred. This, after all, was at the height of the Victorian/Imperial era, and the sons of gentlemen frequently found themselves going overseas in search of opportunity and fortune—or at least wholesomely productive lives—in India or Australia or Canada. This would be the destiny of five of the seven Dickens boys, dispatched young to the army, the navy, the colonies. (Sydney was in the Royal Navy and at sea by the time he was fourteen.) The more adventurous of them took readily to these arrangements, perhaps not realizing that decades could pass before they would see their families again—or that they might die abroad before they could return. The mails were agonizingly slow; there were, of course, no telephones or planes. Emigration was generally permanent.

No one seemed to find these arrangements strange except, perhaps, their mother, and she was not consulted: The law gave fathers complete legal control over their children.

Dickens spent many years, and great pains, to prepare his sons for their future lives. There were endless exchanges with their teachers and tutors and headmasters and clergymen about their education and their abilities. And their own inclinations were consulted and even followed—Sydney, for instance, had wanted the navy since early childhood. The boys were sent to school abroad to improve their languages—French and German were considered essential for careers in business. Plorn (born Edward), the youngest, was sent to agricultural school to prepare him for farming in the Australian outback. Dickens used all his connections and powers of persuasion to further the careers of his sons. He just wouldn't allow them to be indecisive and without occupation, and he just couldn't allow them to stay home and be spendthrift.

In fact, Dickens made very clear, the wholesale dispersal of his sons was in part intended to relieve him of the financial drain involved in supporting the expensive habits of a bunch of young men with no real prospects before them. He's constantly complaining of all the monetary demands on him—not only from the children but from his parents, his brothers and sisters and *their* widows and children; from retainers, connections, friends down on their luck. And after he so brutally dispensed with Catherine in 1858, he was supporting her in a separate comfortable establishment, as well as providing for Ellen Ternan. His income was large, but his responsibilities were large, too. Besides, no one had ever helped *him*.

When we stand back and follow the trajectories of the Dickens children, it's impossible not to sympathize both with his disappointment in most of them and with their own

Charles Dickens

apparently unrealized lives. But that may well be because we can't help seeing these lives through the lens of their father's great expectations for them. Yes, a number of them appear somewhat unfocused, even feckless: In his comprehensive biography, Peter Ackroyd speaks of something "that appeared to make them peculiarly unsuited to the world and to each other." Yet he goes on to suggest that perhaps "we exaggerate their characteristics, just as everything pertaining to Dickens becomes exaggerated; perhaps they were in a sense almost too 'normal,' too little like their father, and have as a result suffered at the hands of disappointed commentators." Certainly, their lives, however unfortunate, were far from disgraceful and would attract no opprobrium (and no attention) if they didn't have the Dickens name attached to them.

Catherine Dickens

There were nine surviving children (Dora was eight months old when she died), and two of the boys died young, Walter in the army in India, Sydney at sea. Both of these young men shared the fatal family weakness of financial irresponsibility—they lived and died in debt—but they were doing well in their professions when they died, and were respected and liked by their colleagues. Charley eventually established himself as an admired editor and man of letters. Henry became a successful, even distinguished, jurist. Kate, the second daughter, had a life filled with conflict but eventually rich in achievement and emotional satisfaction. Her older sister, Mamie, was not a happy woman, and her life took an unhappy turn; no one really understood her. It was the four boys who emigrated whose lives seem to us to have petered out without fulfillment, yet those lives were no more disastrous than most.

It is easy to condemn Dickens as an over-demanding, even harsh, father, but he was also a loving, generous, and involved one. There were rules that had to be followed, mostly to do with neatness, order, punctuality, but he was always available to the children when they needed him: Helping this one overcome a lisp, that one when in need of advice, sitting with them for hours when they were unwell—he was the only one whom Katey, for instance, would allow to be with her when she was dangerously ill. They drew pictures for him; they wrote to him confidingly and he responded fully and sympathetically; they were included in all the fun and games, including the famous home theatricals. He romped with them, took them on long walks—sometimes exhausting them with his preternatural energy. Every Christmas he took them to the famous toy store in Holborn to shop for their presents. He had a special voice for each of them. How could they not adore him? He may have been strict, but they knew he loved them, although direct expressions of love were difficult for him once the children were no longer little. He acknowledged "a habit of suppression . . . which makes me chary of showing my affections, even to my children, except when they are very young."

It cannot have been easy being a child of the man who was not only the world's most famous writer but the world's most beloved writer, and probably the best-known person in the nation apart from the Queen. And it certainly was not easy being caught in the viral family atmosphere after Dickens eliminated his wife from his life and to a considerable extent cut the children off from their mother, whom, despite his disclaimers, they also loved. They were without question damaged by the wreck of their parents' marriage, particularly since there were no softenings of the harsh reality. (After the separation Dickens communicated with his wife only three times in the final twelve years of his life.) The children lived with him and their Aunt Georgina, and although their mother could always see them in her own home, they knew that he disliked it when they visited her. They were forbidden to speak with the rest of her family, including their grandmother, whom Dickens felt had betrayed him. The older ones were torn; the younger ones, confused. None of them was told anything about why their parents had separated—it was never mentioned: One day they lived together as a family, the next day their mother was gone.

But there is something bewildering about them that is not so easy to explain—after all, being the children of a broken marriage is hardly unique. Is it, then, our own great expectations for the Dickens children which have been disappointed? His? Theirs? And what were the arcs and particularities of their lives? We can only hope that they didn't see their lives as disappointments; that they lived them the way we all live our lives—from day to day, doing the best we can. Perhaps in the long run it was easier for some of them to have played out their stories in Australia and Canada and India, where others could more easily forget who their father was and where expectations of them had to do only with how they conducted themselves. When he died, in 1870, they ranged in age from thirty-three to seventeen—Charley an established family man working for his father; Plorn a boy more or less on his own in the outback. Dickens's death freed them all from his immediate influence, but by dividing their individual biographies into two sections—pre- and post-1870—I hope to emphasize that they never really transcended his decisive effect on them.

PART ONE

1837–1870

*From the births of the children
to Dickens's death*

Charley Dickens, painted in 1852 by George Richmond

CHARLEY

Charles Culliford Boz Dickens, 1837–1896

WE CHRISTEN the infant wonder on . . ." "We christen the infant phenomenon on . . ." "We are going to bring within the pale of Christianity on . . ." So Dickens writes to his friends just after January 6, 1837—Twelfth Night—the day his first child, Charley, is born. His tone is jocular, but you can tell from these invitations how excited, gratified, proud he is to be a father; to have a son. Why else give him his own name?

He is almost twenty-five; the mother is twenty-one. Two years earlier he was a minor journalist. Today he is the most successful writer of his time—the author of the overwhelmingly popular *Pickwick Papers*, still being serialized, and already launched on *Oliver Twist*. He's a public sensation, he's good-looking, he's liked, and being comfortably married to a nice, pretty, affectionate girl from a good family has salved the wounds he had suffered during the two years of anguish endured in his fruitless pursuit of Maria Beadnell.

As all the Dickens children will, Charley picks up a silly nickname: he's "Flaster Floby," a corruption of Master Toby.

He's full of feeling and full of fun. When he's four, his father writes to Forster, "I am delighted with Charley's precocity. He takes arter his father, he does." After a visit from Long-fellow, whom the Dickenses had met and liked during their 1842 American tour, Dickens writes to him: "After you left us, Charley invented and rehearsed with his sisters a dramatic scene in your honour, which is still occasionally enacted. It commences with expressive pantomime, and begins immediately after the ceremony of drinking healths. The three small glasses are all raised together, and they look at each other very hard. Then Charley cries, 'Mr. Longfellow! Hoo-ra-a-a-a-a-e!' Two other shrill voices repeat the sentiment, and the little glasses are drained to the bottom. The whole concludes with a violent rapping of the table, and a hideous barking from the little dog, who wakes up for the purpose." Charley is five. When he's six, the family is spending the summer at the East Kent resort town of Broadstairs, where they vacationed by the sea almost annually for twenty years, and Dickens reports to a friend, "Charley is so popular with the boatmen, that I begin to think of Robinson Crusoe, and the propriety of living in-land. I saw him yesterday through a telescope, miles out at sea, steering an enormous fishing smack, to the unspeakable delight of seven gigantic companions, clad in oilskins." A year later, he's at a Christmas party where he "indulged in numerous phases of genteel dissipation." At eight he was busy composing a four-act play whose hero was named Boy.

Before he was ten, "some philanthropist," as he was to write a lifetime later, presented him with a splendid toy theater in which—in a way reminiscent of more modern fathers with their sons' electric trains—Dickens became obsessively interested, his feverish absorption and energy culminating in a glorious spectacle called "The Elephant of Siam." This theater, Charley tells us, then became his again, and "found its way to the nursery, where in process of time a too realistic performance of The Miller and His Men, comprising an injudicious expenditure of gunpowder and red-fire, brought about the catastrophe which finishes the career of most theatres, and very nearly set fire to the house as well."

Well before then Dickens was carefully planning and supervising Charley's education. He had begun with a governess, then had gone to a small local school for half a year before the family moved to Italy, where he was tutored at home, and returned to the school when they came back to England. But what to do now with this high-spirited, bright, and kind boy? The answer came from one of the most remarkable associations of Dickens's life—his friendship with, and semi-professional relationship with, the great heiress Angela Burdett-Coutts, who in 1837, the very year of *Pickwick* and of Charley's birth, inherited her grandfather's banking fortune of almost £3,000,000, making her the richest woman in England. The Queen would eventually make her a baroness in her own right, to honor her philanthropic achievements, and when she died, at the age of ninety-two (having married when she was sixty-nine), she had given away an amount equivalent to her original inheritance—£3,000,000. King Edward VII would remark of her that "after my mother [Queen Victoria], she was the most remarkable woman in the kingdom."

Dickens became Coutts's adviser on her extensive philanthropies—they shared a passionate interest in the poor and abused. She would, through the decades, found or support scores of philanthropic projects, from societies for the prevention of cruelty to children and animals to schools for the poor (the famous Ragged Schools) and the building of churches; from help for Turkish peasants and refugees after the Russo-Turkish war of 1877 to organizations for the aboriginal peoples of Australia and the Dayaks of Borneo; from lifeboats for the fishermen of Brittany to drinking fountains for dogs.

The charity with which Dickens was most deeply involved and which he himself had proposed to Coutts was Urania Cottage, a haven for homeless women, some of questionable morals, who wanted to prepare themselves for useful lives overseas. Dickens threw himself into this project with his usual energy, supervising the construction of the cottage, hiring the staff, overseeing the choice of penitents, advising on the progress of individual cases. His correspondence with Coutts on these matters is astoundingly voluminous and detailed, and suggests two minds in generous sympathy—she, grateful for his practical guidance; he, impressed with her character and her grasp. She was shy, and their relationship was formal, but they understood and trusted each other.

Eager to do something for him in return, since of course his efforts on her behalf were voluntary, she offered to underwrite Charley's education. (She was already sending an elaborate Twelfth Night cake every year to celebrate his birthday.) In response to this munificent offer, Dickens writes to her, "I could do nothing better for him than to accept—I could do nothing half so good for him as to accept—your generous offer. My object is to make him a good man and a wise one; and to place him in the best position I can help him to, for the exercise of his abilities and acquirements. Your help towards such an end is priceless to me, and to him. You could not (but you know it, I am sure) have done a more tender service."

Angela Burdett-Coutts

Charley is eight at this point, and Dickens tells Coutts, "I should not say that in small scholarship, he is very far advanced as yet, for I have been more solicitous, in the first instance, about his health than his study. But he is a child of a very uncommon capacity; and I have no doubt (neither has his present Master) of his rapidly winning his way upward, in any school whatever. His natural talent is quite remarkable."

A few months later, however, he follows up, "We have no reason to think that Charley has anything but a vigorous constitution, and good sound health. But when he is in full school employment, there is a strange kind of *fading* comes over him sometimes; the like of which, I don't think I ever saw . . . [I] am not at all fearful for him, except as I know him to be very quick and sensitive. But I fear if it were to continue, and he were at school at a distance from home, I should have real cause for anxiety; and as you leave the choice to me, I would, solely on this account, prefer King's College, if you think well of it too . . ."

She does think well of it (as if she would possibly have disagreed with Dickens about what was best for his son), and by the time Charley is nine, she is hearing that he "has won a Geneva watch by speaking French in three months. I rashly pledged myself to make that desperate present in the event of his succeeding—and as he has succeeded, I mean to go over to Geneva with him in great state, and endow him with his prize in as solemn a manner as I can possibly confer it." Even at this early date, Dickens is almost unnaturally excited and gratified when one of the children demonstrates ability or success—as if he is already armoring himself against their inevitable failures.

This practice of conferring with Coutts about Charley, informing her of his progress and setbacks, soliciting her opinions, making her, in essence, party to Charley's life as if she were a loving—and rich—aunt, continues through the years in immense detail and intensity. Alas, since Dickens destroyed in enormous bonfires the thousands of letters he had received through the decades, we do not have her responses, but certainly she was caught up in the boy's future, and enjoyed Charley's communications and visits to her. She also was on happy if formal terms with Catherine Dickens. And the opulent Twelfth Night/birthday cakes kept coming. (In 1850, "Charley's cake—a most splendid one—arrived an hour ago. He and his two sisters instantly celebrated the event by putting it on a table and dancing a polka.") One was even delivered by coach across Europe.

Through his letters we have a very full account of Charley's schooling, the high point of which was the stretch, beginning when he was twelve, that he spent at Eton, a place to which Dickens would never have sent him without Coutts's financial backing. When he takes the boy there to be interviewed, Charley is left alone for half an hour with the assistant master, who, Coutts is immediately informed, reports to the father "in high and unqualified terms, that [Charley] had been thoroughly well grounded and well taught—that he had examined him in Virgil and Herodotus, and he not only knew what he was about perfectly well, but showed an intelligence in reference to those authors which did his tutor great credit. He really appeared most interested and pleased, and filled me with a grateful feeling toward you, to whom Charley owes so much."

Charley seems to have done well at school, winning some prizes and at one point "declared at the head of his division." Dickens was clearly pleased at having his oldest boy at Eton, and enjoyed visiting him there. In 1851, for instance (Charley is fourteen), he reports to a friend:

Let me tell you that a week or so ago, I took Charley and three of his schoolfellows down the river, gipseying . . . accompanied by two immense hampers from Fortnum and Mason's, on (I believe) the wettest morning ever seen out of the tropics. It cleared before we got to Slough . . . When the first hamper came out of the luggage-van, I was conscious of their dancing behind the Guard. And when the second came out—with bottles in it—they all stood wildly on one leg. We then got out a couple of flies to drive to the boathouse. I put them in the first, but they couldn't sit still a moment, and were perpetually flying up and down, like the toy-figures in the sham snuff boxes. In this order we went to "Tom Brown's the tailor's" where they all dressed in aquatic costume . . . We embarked—the sun shining now—in a galley with a striped awning, which I had ordered for the purpose, and all rowing hard went down the river. We dined in a field. What I suffered for fear those boys should get drunk—the struggles I underwent in a contest of feeling between hospitality and prudence—must ever remain untold. I feel, even now, old with anxiety of that tremendous hour. They were very good, however. The speech of one became thick, and his eyes too like the lobster's to be comfortable, but only temporarily. He recovered, and I suppose outlived the Salad he took. I have heard nothing to the contrary, and imagine I should have been implicated on the Inquest if there had been one. We had tea and rashers of bacon at a public house, and came home, the last five or six miles, in a prodigious thunderstorm . . . The getting wet was the culminating point of the entertainments. You never in your life beheld such objects as they were—and their perfect unconsciousness that it was at all advisable to go home and change, or that there was anything to prevent their standing at the Station two mortal hours to see me off, was wonderful.

This was the boyhood Dickens himself had never enjoyed, and he reveled in it. (Years later, a participant in another such picnic would write, "What a day that was! The great man was full of life, bubbling over with fun, the youngest boy of the party . . . the spirit of joy incarnate.") We can't help noticing how he immediately turns it all into a comic sketch, as if it's Boz who's observing, not a father who's participating. But how can we blame him for being himself? It seems at times that nothing is real for him until he's written it down.

Although he's generally pleased with Charley, the habitual ominous note sounds. During the summer holidays of 1851, Dickens informs Coutts, "He is very much grown—an excellent boy at home, and as good to his brothers and sisters as if he had never been away. All he wants, is a habit of perseverance. With that, he could do any thing. He wants it as a fixed purpose and habit of nature. He gets on at Eton, with credit, so easily that he merely takes short rides on his Pegasus and jumps off again, when he ought to be putting him at great leaps." His tutor had "much commended" him, but had previously reported him "rather lazy."

At the end of the following summer—he's fifteen—the serious question arises: What's to become of him? "I had a long talk with Charley . . . in which he behaved in such a manly manner and shewed himself to be such a fine fellow, that he rather disturbed my judicial equanimity. He told me that he would certainly like the Army. I told him, in return, that he must consider the practical difficulties and drawbacks of the life, as well as the bright side. I set both fairly before him, and he then said he would like time to consider, as he would wish to understand himself and do the right. So I settled to go and take a walk with him next month & decide the question in a perfectly open and unreserved confidence. He is the best of boys now, and I hope will not be among any but the best of men."

When they resumed their discussions, he reports to Coutts, Charley "came to the conclusion that he would rather be a merchant, and try to establish some good house of business, where he might find a path perhaps for his younger brothers, and stay at home, and make himself the head of that long, small procession. I was very much pleased with him indeed; he shewed a fine sense and a fine feeling in the whole matter. We have arranged therefore, that he shall leave Eton at Christmas and go to Germany after the holidays to become well acquainted with that language—now most essential in such a walk of life as he will probably tread." This, of course, is Dickens's account of things. One can't help wondering how cheerfully Charley himself welcomed being sent off to Germany to learn the language, leaving behind the gratifications of his life with his peers at Eton.

Dickens gets help from his German publisher in finding a place for Charley in a professor's home in Leipzig, where he would "live happily; would obtain a scholarly knowledge of German and French (of the latter he knows a great deal already); would be overlooked and taken care of as every boy requires to be; and would not lose what he had already learned." In another letter, to the German professor, he stipulates, "I wish him to be not too obviously restrained, and to

have the advantages of cheerful and good society . . . I want
him to have an interest in, and to acquire a knowledge of the
life around him, and to be treated like a gentleman though
pampered in nothing. By punctuality in all things great and
small, I set great store." The professor in due course comes to
like and appreciate the boy, finds him "much improved in
many little things that displeased" him at first, "but has doubts
about his desire to study" and "is not quite certain that to be
a merchant, is his earnest and fast determination."

In reporting all this to Coutts, Dickens goes on to give his
own observations of his son.

He is very gentle and affectionate, particularly fond of his
sisters, very happy in their society, and very desirous to
win the love of those who are dear to him. His inclinations are all good; but I think he has less fixed purpose
and energy than I could have supposed possible in my son.
He is not aspiring, or imaginative in his own behalf. With
all the tenderer and better qualities which he inherits
from his mother, he inherits an indescribable lassitude of
character—a very serious thing in a man—which seems
to me to express the want of a strong compelling hand
always beside him. Nothing but the conviction formed in
his infancy that it *must be done*, renders him attentive to
the little points of punctuality and order required of him
at home. I believe him to have fewer active faults than
ninety nine boys out of a hundred at his age; but his vir-
tues and merits all want activity, too.

Father and son have another long talk, and Dickens again
advises against the army ("a poor pursuit for a young man of

no property"), doubting that it "would bring him to much self-respect, contentment, or happiness, in middle life." There are further talks (all reported at great length to Coutts), and the decision is made: Charley will pursue his mercantile career, returning to Germany for a time, and meanwhile going down to the offices of Dickens's immensely popular magazine, *Household Words*, where, Dickens writes to Arthur Ryland, a businessman friend of his in Birmingham, "I find him very quick, with natural facility of writing systematic and terse letters, and with a considerable power (unusual at his age) of abstracting the pith of any documents from a mass of words."

At the same time, Dickens is making thorough inquiries among his many connections about potential jobs in the mercantile world. Ryland's advice is solicited, as is that of a Mr. Bates at Barings House in London. Both men point out the difficulties Charley will encounter, and stress the determination and hard work essential to his making his way. "I have pointed out to Charley the kind of drudgery essential to the calling (but without saying that I think it will scarcely call into action the best sort of power he possesses—though I have a misgiving on that head), and have told him to think again and be certain he is still in earnest."

We may fault Dickens for his over-negative view of his boys, but no one can fault him for neglecting his responsibilities toward them: For twenty years he exhausted himself trying to strengthen their willpower and forward their careers. But could he really have believed that Charley's temperament and capacities were particularly suitable to a mercantile career? Why didn't it occur to Dickens that his son's demonstrated aptitude for the work at *Household Words* might be a strong signal as to where his happiest future might lie?

Charley launched himself into the world of commerce with the hope of forming a partnership with some other congenial young man, but his various efforts came to nothing. Bad luck, bad timing, bad choices combined to block his efforts, which were certainly real but undoubtedly less forceful than his father would have preferred. It cannot have helped that in 1858, the very moment when he was attempting to establish himself, came the domestic crisis that shattered the Dickens family and placed Charley in particular in a miserable position. Living with Catherine had become insupportable to Dickens, and since he could never acknowledge bad behavior on his own part, he—first privately, then publicly—denounced her as an impossible wife for him and mother for their children: If he could convince others (and himself) that she was indeed an unloving and unloved woman, he would be justified in casting her out of his life.

Anyone who tried to reason with him, or to defend Catherine, was expelled into utter darkness, never to be forgiven. Only Miss Coutts, who gently tried to get him to rethink his actions, was tolerated, though their relationship suffered, too, and quietly petered out. Considering how he venerated her and how much he owed her, it is a telling sign that even she could not get him to reconsider his behavior.

The children, he determined, would continue to live with him and their Aunt Georgina, although, as we have seen, Catherine was grudgingly permitted to see them. The younger ones (Plorn was only six) didn't understand what was happening, but the three oldest—Charley and his two sisters—understood all too well.

Naturally, Charley had been shocked when he heard of his mother's dismissal, but after considering the new situation, he wrote to his father that he had decided it was his duty to accompany his mother into exile. "Don't suppose that in making my choice, I was actuated by any feeling of preference for my mother to you. God knows I love you dearly, and it will be a hard day for me when I have to part with you and the girls. But in doing as I have done, I hope I am doing my duty, and you will understand it so." Dickens, in his less than honest way, would suggest that it was he who had urged Charley to take up residence with Catherine, but that was not the case. This was Charley's finest hour—we can only imagine the psychic cost to him of defying his father on so crucial a matter. Fortunately, after he moved out, his good nature made it easy for him to maintain affectionate relations with Dickens and to visit the rest of the family frequently.

At the time when he moved from his father's house to Catherine's, he was employed quite successfully at Barings, a major financial institution in the City. His previous trial employment at a broker's office had resulted in his employers giving him "so high a character for zeal and ability" that Barings felt it would be "unfair" for him to begin as a volunteer, and they started him off with a salary of £50 a year; quickly he earned a bonus of £10 and an increase of salary as well. But what he wanted was to find an overseas connection and set up as a merchant on his own. In 1860 he sailed for Hong Kong, "strongly backed up by Barings, to buy tea on his own account."

The tea business did not work out, nor did a paper-mill business backed by Coutts—it went bankrupt, and Dickens wouldn't or couldn't come to the financial rescue. "My boy Charles," he wrote in mid-1868 to James Fields, his American publisher and friend, "who went into a paper making company with the very identical men against whom I wrote him a most earnest warning when he married, has come to grief in connexion with that precious firm, and staggers back . . . on the paternal shoulder. I am at my wits' end to know what to do." But he *did* know what to do, taking Charley into the offices of his second tremendously successful magazine, *All the Year Round*. W. H. Wills, his brilliant sub-editor and close friend, was clearly never going to recover well enough from a serious riding accident to resume his arduous duties, and Dickens thought that Charley could take over some of his responsibilities. "I must turn his education to the best account I can until we can hit upon some other start in life, and he can certainly take the bag [of unsolicited mail] and report on its contents, and carry on the correspondence."

This was work that, as it turned out and could have been predicted, was well-suited to Charley, and he slowly took over all of Wills's duties until his father formally named him sub-editor. (We may ask ourselves again why Dickens hadn't recognized his affinity for literary journalism earlier on and pointed Charley in its direction: Clearly, he was more suited to the world of literature than to commerce or the army.)

And then, in a codicil to his will, written just before his death, Dickens left Charley his share and financial interest in *All the Year Round*—a last-minute gesture of approval, perhaps, or a last-minute rescue operation. Which Charley was certainly in need of, as by this time he was not only a husband but the father of six children, with two more to come (of the eight, seven were girls).

Leaving his father's home in favor of Catherine's hadn't been Charley's only gesture of independence. In a farcical yet unpleasant contretemps involving Dickens, Thackeray, and Dickens's protégé Edmund Yates, Charley took Thackeray's side, and Dickens retaliated by blackballing his son's petition to join the Garrick Club. "The poor boy," said Thackeray, "is very much cast down at his father's proceedings."

But Charley's ultimate defiance of his father lay in his choice of a wife. Bessie Evans was the daughter of Dickens's old publisher Frederick Evans, with whom he had had a close relationship until Evans didn't prove ardent enough in his rejection of Catherine after the break. For Dickens, such moderation inevitably resulted in eternal resentment—"hatred" is not too strong a word—and permanent banishment inevitably followed. Evans became a non-person, and Dickens violently disapproved of Charley's choice of Bessie. To Mrs. Hannah Brown, Coutts's friend and companion, he wrote, "I wish I could hope that Charley's marriage may not be a disastrous one. There is no help for it, and the dear fellow does what is unavoidable—his foolish mother would have effectually committed him if nothing else had; chiefly, I suppose because her hatred of the bride and all belonging to her, used to know no bounds, and was quite inappeasable. But I have a strong belief, founded on careful observation of him, that he cares nothing for the girl."

This ugly and deluded version of reality is yet another symptom of the derangement of mind and spirit that Dickens was undergoing at this period of his life. Charley and Bessie had been crazy about each other since childhood, and their marriage, despite the vicissitudes they were to encounter, would be a long and happy one. Their oldest daughter, Mary Angela Dickens, would one day write, "It was a family joke—and also a fact!—that he and my mother were engaged when she was seven years old! They were lovers all their life."

The one immediate benefit of Dickens's grotesque behavior was that since going to the wedding would have involved entering the Evans home, he refused to attend, as a result of which Catherine was able to witness the marriage of her first child. It should be noted, however, that he remained kind, even loving, to Bessie herself, as well as to the six children she bore Charley before Dickens's death. They were frequently at Gad's Hill, and as always he enjoyed the company of little ones—the younger the better. What he didn't enjoy was the appellation "grandfather"—all reminders of his aging distressed him—so he had the children address him as "Venerables" instead.

Charley's equable and generous disposition helped him withstand the buffeting his father had subjected him to through the years of repeated failures, and he remained loving and supportive until the very end. He could recall the countless happy times, even in the midst of the unhappy times. He remembered not only the schoolboy jaunts at Eton but the years in Europe, "walks along the lake-side or among the beautiful hills behind the town [Lausanne], or visits to open air fetes in the heart of the green woods where he was always anxious that I should join and distinguish myself in the boyish sports that were going on . . ." And, later, in Paris, accompanying his father to a "good many theatres to 'consolidate my French.'" And "continual excursions and picnics . . . constant impromptu dances, and games, and forfeits, and such like diversions; performances of conjuring tricks with my father as the magician . . ."

Perhaps most important to him were the decades of amateur and semi-professional theatricals that Charley loved as much as his father did, participating in them from his earliest childhood. A week before Dickens died, Charley was backstage at some dramatic presentation "ringing all the bells and working all the lights . . . with infectious enjoyment." His love for the theater would last his lifetime.

In Dickens's final two years, Charley was not only the mainstay at the office but a constantly attentive and concerned son. His father's health was by now precarious—he had utterly compromised it in the demanding public readings that he performed throughout Great Britain and on the near-fatal American tour of 1867–1868. It was during these last years that he determined to add his terrifying reading of Bill Sikes's murder of Nancy to his program. Charley was to recall witnessing his father, outdoors at Gad's Hill, "striding up and down, gesticulating wildly, and, in the character of Mr. Sikes, murdering Nancy with every circumstance of the most aggravated brutality." Later that day, Dickens read him the entire scene. "The finest thing I have ever heard," was his verdict, "but don't do it"—a verdict confirmed by John Forster and others. But Dickens would never be guided by others.

The performances of the murder were so powerful and so demanding that Dickens's health rapidly deteriorated further, until under unambiguous orders from his doctors, he brought them to an end in April 1869. But he felt obligated to fulfill a commitment for a final dozen performances the following year. "I have had some steps put up against the side of the platform, Charley," said one of Dickens's doctors, who was in constant attendance. "You must be there every night, and if you see your father falter in the least, you must run up and catch him and bring him off with me, or, by Heaven, he'll die before them all."

"What I felt during those readings, and when I saw the exhausted state of the reader in his dressing-room afterwards," wrote Charley many years later, "I need not tell you." That was in March 1870, and three months later his father was dead.

Charley was to write of

the last time I was with him before he lay dying in the dining-room at Gadshill . . . He was in town for our usual Thursday meeting on the business of "All the Year Round," and, instead of returning to Gadshill on that day had remained over night, and was at work again in his room in Wellington Street, on the Friday, the 3rd of June. During the morning I had hardly seen him except to take his instructions about some work I had to do, and at about one o'clock—I had arranged to go into the country for the afternoon—I cleared up my table and prepared to leave. The door of communication between our rooms was open, as usual, and, as I came towards him, I saw that he was writing very earnestly. After a moment I said: "If you don't want anything more, sir, I shall be off now," but he continued his writing with the same intensity as before, and gave no sign of being aware of my presence. Again I spoke—louder, perhaps, this time— and he rested his head and looked at me long and fixedly. But I soon found that, although his eyes were bent upon me and he seemed to be looking at me earnestly, he did not see me, and that he was, in fact, unconscious for the moment of my very existence. He was in Dreamland with Edwin Drood, and I left him—for the last time.

When several days later Dickens suffered his stroke at Gad's Hill, Charley rushed from London to find him unconscious. As he sat with his sisters waiting for their father to die, the heavy scent of syringa floated through the open windows. He was never able to bear their scent again.

MAMIE

Mary Angela Dickens, 1838–1896

FROM DICKENS to Richard Bentley, March 6, 1838: "My Dear Sir, We were all right here at One o 'Clock this morning when I had an installment of posterity in the shape of a daughter." The daughter was Mary Angela Dickens, named for the adored Mary who had died less than a year earlier in the same house on Doughty Street where the new baby was born. This new-born Mary was "Mamie" (or Mamey) from the start, and always, although Dickens sometimes referred to her by her given name in formal correspondence. Perhaps "Mary" was a name too sacred to Dickens for everyday use.

"It would be difficult to find a more attractive girl than 'Mamie' Dickens," wrote Percy Fitzgerald in his *Memories of Charles Dickens*, published in 1913. "Decidedly pretty she was, but her power lay in her interesting character—its curious spirit of *independence* and haughty refusal of submission, which made one think that some Petruchio might arrive and confront this imperious being." It's not surprising that Fitzgerald remembered her this way: He had been an ardent

Mamie Dickens

suitor for her hand during the 1860s and, unlike a previous suitor, had her father's full backing. The imperious Mamie, however, wasn't interested.

Of all the Dickens children, she is the hardest to grasp, the most contradictory, and possibly the least happy. Yet she started off with everything in her favor, including what at first seemed an appealingly gentle nature—her father's nickname for her was "Mild Glo'ster." It was Katey, a year younger, who would be known for her fiery temper.

Mamie, born just fourteen months after Charley, spent her childhood performing all the tasks appropriate to a well-bred Victorian girl. She played the piano adequately if not especially well; she was too shy, she said, to perform for company, but she loved to please her father in later years by playing his favorites for him in the evenings—"ballads, national airs, lively dances, Mendelssohn, Chopin, Mozart." She arranged flowers prettily. She learned the arts of housekeeping. She was a very effective participant in the Dickens family theatricals—at another time and in a different society she might have found herself as an actress. She spoiled her pets. And her father indulged her, although she too had to keep everything in perfect order. As she wrote in her short and unrevealing memoir of him, he "encouraged us in every possible way to make ourselves useful, and to adorn and beautify our rooms with our own hands, and to be ever tidy and neat . . . Even in those early days, he made a point of visiting every room in the house once a morning, and if a chair was out of its place, or a blind not quite straight, or a crumb left on the floor, woe betide the offender."

Dickens was at his warmest in letters to the children, with birthdays especially marked by charming notes when he was away. When Mamie is about to turn eleven he writes to her, "My Dearest Mamey. I am not engaged on the evening of your birthday. But even if I had an engagement of the most particular kind, I should excuse myself from keeping it, so that I might have the pleasure of celebrating at home, and among my children, the day that gave me such a dear and good daughter as you." Since, as we have noted, late in his life he burned all the letters, from whatever source, that he had received, we lack Mamie's side of the correspondence, but one of his to her, written when she was nine, suggests the affection and mutual trust between them: "My dearest Mamey, I am delighted to hear that you are going to improve in your spelling, because no one can write properly without spelling well. But I know you will learn whatever you are taught, because you are always good, industrious, and attentive. That is what I always say of my Mamey. The note you sent me this morning is a very nice one, and the spelling is beautiful. Always, my dear Mamey, Your affectionate Papa."

He is anxious about her health, always fragile—she almost died of cholera when she was sixteen—yet she was regularly on the go, the first young woman in the neighborhood, for instance, to ride a bicycle; later, going off with friends on fishing expeditions. ("My daughter Mary has been fishing for trout in Scotland—it is unnecessary to add has caught none.") But as time passed, she began to attract from her father the same kind of dispassionate criticism that Charley and the other boys regularly received. Arthur Adrian, in *Georgina Hogarth and the Dickens Circle*, puts it this way: "For all Mamie's agreeable and docile qualities and for all her father's indulgence of her, it seems probable that, had she been a boy, her lack of decision and practical industry might have evoked the same censure Dickens bestowed upon his sons. When she revealed herself at times to be as vaguely passive and unpurposeful as her mother, he was not known to cloak his annoyance under the same sort of badinage he had used in referring to Catherine."

It cannot have helped that Mamie bore a decided resemblance to her mother, a resemblance noted by many people, including Hans Christian Andersen when he paid a visit to the family in 1857. Henry James, on the other hand, in later years found her "Ladylike (in black silk and black lace) and the image of her father." Mamie was considered attractive. Percy Fitzgerald would note her "petite figure, small, well-

Mamie Dickens

shaped features . . . and ready wit." Gladys Storey, the great friend of Katey's old age, wrote of Mamie in *Dickens and Daughter*, "she was very pretty and dainty, always tastefully dressed, and had a soft way of speaking." Annie Fields found her "very lady-like and pretty . . . mild, quiet and attentive," but less distinctive than her sister, Katey; "more like other people."

Yet she was also willful, and increasingly so as time passed. Like other young women she enjoyed parties and balls, and more and more she yearned for the social life of

London. To satisfy her, Dickens—now permanently resident at Gad's Hill—would rent a house every year in town so that she could enjoy the "season." But once he had eliminated Catherine from his life in 1858, when Mamie was twenty, the social status of the girls was somewhat undermined. There was a scandalous element to the new domestic arrangements: Mrs. Dickens was in exile and the girls were living with their father, not, as would be proper, with their mother; worse, they were also living with Aunt Georgie, their mother's unmarried sister. Everyone's sympathies (except Dickens's) were with the well-liked and inoffensive if unexciting Catherine; no one really believed his public accusations that she was an incompetent housewife and a lazy, cold, and indifferent mother. One view of the situation, expressed with her customary incisiveness and asperity, appeared in a letter (reprinted in Susan M. Rossi-Wilcox's *Dinner for Dickens*) from the imposing sociologist and feminist Harriet Martineau, who contributed frequently to *Household Words*:

About the Dickens case,—I will just say that my rejoicing in the domestic happiness I formerly heard so much of from their intimates was deepened by some surprise;—so that I am not so wholly confounded at this manifestation as many people are. I mean that always, from the observation of a long life, I distrust such an amount of *sentimentality*, combined with selflove in the husband, as has always existed in the D household. Moreover, amidst it all, he openly & thoroughly regarded his wife as "his woman"; provided another to take care of the children & walk with him, when Mrs D. was unable,—which she usually was;—chose her to dress in black velvet, & sit at her embroidery, at leisure *for him*, & so on. After this sort of life,—now, when she has borne him above a dozen children (9 living) & the time for collapse has come,—exhaustion, indifference, indolence &c, is she to be turned adrift because she is (if she is) subject to that *fretfulness & jealousy* which are the *specific results* of such a life as he has chosen that her's shd be?—And not a daughter has she with her!—only that weak son.

When Dickens insisted that his daughters remain with him after the break, they acquiesced. Katey seems to have been torn—after all, her brother Charley had chosen to live with Catherine, and it would have been natural for the younger daughter to attend her mother, just as it might be seen as natural for the elder to take over the household in the absence of her mother. Katey was able to extricate herself from the situation only by escaping into marriage. But Mamie made it absolutely clear from the start that she chose her father. During these painful years—from 1858 to 1870—she simply stayed away from Catherine, happy to be "Miss Dickens," her father's official hostess and housekeeper, although it was obvious that Georgie was really in charge.

Unfortunately, this irregular arrangement led to a considerable amount of criticism of father and daughters and to a subtle social ostracizing. As one of Catherine's relatives who was hardly disinterested but who seems to have been clear-headed put it, "they, poor girls, have also been flattered as being taken notice of as the daughters of a popular writer. He, too, is a caressing father and indulgent in trifles, and they in their ignorance of the world, look no further nor are aware of the injury he does them."

Before Kate's marriage, both girls had been exhibiting a febrile nervousness in public. A malicious letter to the publisher John Blackwood from a critic who was also a friend of the family suggests the atmosphere: "His daughters—now under the benign wing of their aunt, Miss Hogarth—are not received into society. You would be excessively amused if you heard all the gigantic efforts of the family to keep their foot in the world—how they call upon people they never called on before & and that they have treated with the most dire contempt. Fancy Dickens & his family going to call on that worthy couple—Mr. & Mrs. Pecksniff, & informing these people upon whom they never called before that they would be happy to see them at Tavistock House. But still better—fancy Pecksniff & his wife in a high moral transport and religious spite informing Miss Hogarth & the Miss Dickenses, that it was with Mrs. Dickens they were acquainted, that if Mrs. Dickens were at Tavistock House they should be happy to call, but otherwise—afraid—very sorry . . ." (The man referred to as Mr. Pecksniff here, a Mr. Hall, was the presumed model for the hypocritical Pecksniff in *Martin Chuzzlewit*).

Although Mamie was Dickens's official hostess, she spent a good deal of her life away from him and Gad's Hill. Her time in London was of increasing importance to her. Georgina reported her as "very gay—out every night—and not at all tired of it." After Dickens, early in 1870, made a command appearance at Buckingham Palace (Queen Victoria was a great admirer), Mamie was invited to the Queen's drawing-room and to a Court ball, so she had the satisfaction of being persona grata on the most exalted social level of all, whatever the gossips were saying. And she had friends everywhere, to whom she would make extended visits. There were the fishing friends in Scotland and the Whites on the Isle of Wight. There were the Humphreys, he a sporting Tory MP. In 1865, Mamie went down to Hampshire to canvass for him in an election campaign. Dickens was only partly amused: "Think of my feelings as a Radical parent! The wrong-headed member and his wife are the friends with whom she hunts, and she helps him to receive (and *de*ceive) the voters, which is very awful!"

Most important of her friends were the remarkable Lehmanns, one of the most attractive and admired couples in London's well-to-do artistic circles. Frederick Lehmann was a successful businessman and politician from a family of German-Jewish artists—his father and uncle had been prominent portrait painters in France, part of the group that included Lizst, Marie d'Agoult, Ingres, et al. Nina Lehmann was the daughter of Robert Chambers, a leading literary figure of Edinburgh, who had conceived of and owned *Chambers's Encyclopedia*, a highly popular and lucrative reference book. She herself was a superb pianist, and close to many of the major musicians of her time, from Pauline Viardot to the great violinist Joachim.

Nina was also by all accounts, and from the evidence of her enchanting letters, a loving and lovable woman, adored by everyone in her circle from Robert Browning to Wilkie Collins (he called her Padrona). She was close to the Dickens family through her Aunt Janet, who was married to W. H. Wills, the man whose physical disabilities had led to Charley Dickens being taken into *All the Year Round*. (The distinction of the family continued into the third generation, with Nina and Frederick's grandchildren, the writers Rosamond and John Lehmann and their sister, the actress Beatrix Lehmann, enjoying distinguished careers through much of the twentieth century.)

For many years Mamie was part of the Lehmanns' innermost circle, not only staying with them for long stretches but frequently traveling with Nina, both at home and abroad. It's from the letters between Nina and Frederick—frequently separated by circumstance, they were in constant correspondence, telling each other everything—that we get our clearest sense of how Mamie appeared to the world in the mid-sixties, when she was approaching thirty and Katey was unhappily married to Charlie Collins, Wilkie's brother.

After a dinner party in 1866 that Nina was unable to attend, Frederick wrote to her:

My dear, anything more demented and awful I have never witnessed. We were fourteen, ten at one table and four at a side table. Chorley [the host], Mamie, Mrs. Vivian and Mr. Underwood at the side table, from which Mamie kept darting distressed and furious glances and shaping her mouth all the time for the word "beast" whenever Chorley looked away from her . . . [Katey] told me that Mamie, who looked round and matronlike, was to be pitied and [that she herself] could not lead such a life, but added mysteriously, "she takes her happiness when she can, and a few visits to town lately have given her all she cares for." She added, "Of course, it will come out. Sure to." My dear, these two girls are going to the devil as fast as can be. From what I hear from third parties who don't know how intimate we are with them, society is beginning to fight very shy of them, particularly Kitty C . . . Mamie may blaze up like a firework any day. Kitty is burning away both character and I fear health slowly but steadily . . . [the others] behaved like a set of maniacs, especially the society women . . . the Dickens and Collins faction was at one end of the drawing-room and Society at the other and when I came up Mamie said the Society women were beasts and the little rooms were suffocating and I was not at all sure I was not in Bedlam.

It was at about this time that, as Wilkie reported to Frederick Lehmann, who passed the news on to Nina, "Mamie who is staying with the Forsters has *dyed* her hair the fashionable colour yellow with a dash of auburn red. What do you say to that?"

Henry Chorley, the host of this awkward dinner party and a notable eccentric, was a prolific and respected writer, probably England's most influential music critic. He was a close friend of the Dickens family and another of Mamie's admirers, although thirty years her senior. (Which may explain why she was mouthing the word "beast" behind his back.) He never ceased caring for her, and at his death, in 1872, he left her an annuity of £200 a year.

It is difficult to gauge Mamie's interest in marriage and/or men in general. There are suggestions that, early on, she was attracted to one young man, but Dickens disapproved and she gave him up—if, indeed, things got to that point. Percy Fitzgerald was a good-looking, ambitious young man involved with *All the Year Round* whose suit Dickens enthusiastically encouraged, but Mamie was dead set against him. (Her father was "grievously disappointed.") In 1868 she attracted the attentions of a very presentable military officer, William Lynch, seven years her senior, a brigade major who was posted at Chatham, near Gad's Hill. Again, her father approved: "I am sorry that Mary will not meet Lynch at St. James's Hall on Tuesday night." (Dickens was giving a reading there.) Georgina writes to Annie Fields about the Lynch possibility, "but

I am afraid to allow myself to be hopeful about it. If only Mamie could share her father's warmth for this perceptive young officer!" After Dickens's death, Lynch wrote a kind letter of condolence to Georgina, who was still regretting that nothing had come of his interest in her niece. "*That*, as you know, was a disappointment to me, and I have never been able to understand how it was that it fell to the ground." But the reason clearly lay in Mamie's strong disinclination to leave Dickens's home in any permanent way, despite her father's and aunt's eagerness to see her married.

There have been suggestions that Mamie had lesbian tendencies—based not only on vague rumors from her later life but on a curious passage in a letter Nina Lehmann wrote to her husband, in which she describes how Mamie, arriving for a visit, greeted her like a "lover," with exaggerated kisses and caresses. Nina was baffled and embarrassed, yet this odd incident did not interrupt their friendship or their frequent holiday trips together. As Lucinda Hawksley wonders in her biography of Katey, is this the nature of the behavior Katey was referring to in her cryptic remark about Mamie's taking her happiness when she can?

Well after Dickens's death, Georgina was still writing about Mamie's marriage prospects to Annie Fields: "I wish she would make such happiness [as Katey's] for herself! although I would miss her sadly, still it would make her happier if she *filled up her life* as she ought to have done. She would be such a good wife and mother! But I fear she is not likely now, to marry."

Her fears were prophetic. Mamie knew what she didn't want. As she put it in a letter to Annie, "It is a glorious inheritance to have such blood flowing in one's veins. I am so glad I never changed my name."

KATEY

Catherine Macready Dickens, 1839–1929

O N OCTOBER 29, 1839, Charles and Catherine celebrated the birth of their third child within three years. Or rather Charles celebrated it and Catherine survived it—her births were always difficult, and as usual it took her weeks, even months, to recover her physical and emotional energies. "Thank God it is now all safely over, and that Kate and the child—another little girl—as well as possible," Dickens wrote at once to Forster.

Named after her mother, baby Catherine—Katey—was soon given her nickname: "Lucifer Box." A "lucifer" was a safety match, and from her earliest years Katey's temper would flare up the way matches flared up—and the way her father's did as well. (Remember: Mamie was labeled Mild Glo'ster.) Like her father she was bright, quick, impetuous, prone to illness, and emotionally up and down—you could almost say manic and depressive. Charles adored her; everyone understood that she was his favorite. Lucinda Hawksley (who happens to be her great-great-great-niece) points out in *Katey* that when writing to Catherine for news of the little

Katey Dickens

ones, her father spells her name in capital letters; the others have to make do with upper- and lower-case. And writing of the children to his brother-in-law, he puts her name first, not in its chronological place. Later, when the children were older and often nervous of their often irascible father, it was always Katey who was sent into his study to ask for a favor or plead for an amnesty, while the others waited outside the door. Mamie herself would write, "And here I would like to correct an error concerning myself. I have been spoken of as my father's 'favourite daughter.' If he had a favourite daughter—and I hope and believe that the one was as dear to him as the other—my dear sister must claim that honour."

She was thought to be the most like him in temperament, even to look the most like him, of all the children. An American friend remembered that "no one of his family seemed to enjoy his humour as much as Kate, and in her quick perception of it she was more like him than the others."

Her childhood, like Mamie's, was the standard Victorian childhood of girls of their class: they shared nurses, governesses, lessons in history and botany, in drawing and singing and dancing, in French and Italian. There was lots of fun as well—the annual holidays at the beach at Broadstairs and outdoor games and indoor treats at home. Katey would recall how "Dickens frequently drove with his girls to Hampstead Heath, where they alighted and romped in the lanes around Jack Straw's Castle, or wandered on either side of him—listening to the stories he had to tell from the storehouse of his wonderful imagination." There were long stays in Europe.

In 1844, however, Katey, not yet five, fell seriously ill in Italy: first, a terrible sore throat, then a growth on the side of her neck that grew larger and larger, and was frighteningly painful—her screams were unbearable. And, as Hawksley puts it, "She didn't want the desperate ministrations of her mother, or those of her capable aunt or the comfortable governess, she wanted her father. Moreover, with a force of character that would remain with her into cantankerous octogenarianism, she *insisted* upon being nursed by her father." Dickens set aside his work—he was starting on *Dombey and Son*—and nursed her. He even tried to mesmerize her (his latest preoccupation)—it had worked with Mamie. But it didn't with Katey. (He concluded that they were too much alike in temperament.) Doctors have offered a number of possible diagnoses, ranging from tuberculosis of the neck (scrofula) to diphtheria to a quinsy—a kind of abscess that can result when severe tonsillitis leads to a dangerous infection—but no one back then was sure what it was. It was months before she was fully recovered, and she emerged from the ordeal painfully thin and too weak to walk. All through this frightening time her father tended to her, writing proudly to a friend, "She would let nobody touch her; in the way of dressing her neck or giving her physic; when she was ill; but her Papa. So I had a pretty tough time of it. But her sweet temper was wonderful to see."

Apart from her consistently delicate health, it sounds like an idyllic childhood, but her parents' marriage was beginning to fray. Hawksley speculates about what Katey called her "superstitions."

> Her brothers would often tease her about her need to touch certain pieces of furniture exactly the same number of times every day and to check under her bed each night before getting into it . . . This behaviour seems to suggest that Katey was troubled as a young child and felt the need to control those things she could—like the number of times she touched each piece of furniture—as a way of dispelling her feelings about the things she couldn't control; such as her parents' deteriorating marriage and her father's irritation with her mother.

Today, as Hawksley points out, such behavior in a child would be identified as obsessive-compulsive disorder and treated with psychotherapy or medication. In Katey's day, it would have appeared as a puzzling eccentricity.

Dickens was close to a number of well-known artists, and Katey was familiar with them and their work. By the time she was eleven, her drawing was showing real ability, and when she was thirteen her father enrolled her in the recently established Bedford College in Bedford Square, the first educational establishment in Britain to offer a university education to women. (It was also the first art college to offer life-drawing classes to women.) Katey joined in 1853 and spent five or so years studying there, progressing from drawing to oil painting, presumably preparing herself for portraiture, at which she would later enjoy a successful career.

She was also growing into an attractive young woman—and at fifteen and sixteen she developed a serious crush on her father's young protégé Edmund Yates, who was more interested in impressing the father than the daughter. (Besides, he was married.) She also involved herself more wholeheartedly than she ever had before in the annual family theatricals. (Yates was in attendance.) There was a scare when she fell badly ill again; happily, it was a violent case of whooping cough, not the diphtheria they feared. The high point of these late adolescent years was the seven-month period the family spent in Paris, where Mamie and Katey shared art lessons with their great friends Anny and Minny Thackeray, daughters of the novelist, and where Katey watched the famous artist Ary Scheffer paint Charles's portrait. When she was seventeen, back in London, she performed at home in the drama *The Frozen Deep*, which Wilkie Collins had just written, as well as in the accompanying farce. She was billed as "Miss Kate."

It was after *The Frozen Deep* had been performed privately a number of times (including, by royal request, for Queen Victoria) that Dickens decided to show it to the public, and employed professionals to replace Katey and the other girls, since of course well-bred young women could not appear as actresses in the commercial theater. It was then, in the summer of 1857, that he met the eighteen-year-old Ellen Ternan. His passion for her—combined with his increasing dissatisfaction with (in fact, aversion to) his wife—is what led him to the most extreme action of his life: the public and humiliating dismissal of Catherine from his home. As we know, the callous way he treated her astonished the world, horrified most of his friends, and ruptured the lives of his children.

Since he had complete legal control over them, he could and did insist on keeping the younger ones with him, but the oldest three were on the cusp of adulthood, with some freedom of choice. While Charley bravely decided to remain with his victimized mother and Mamie had no difficulty about staying with her adored father, Katey, perhaps closest of them all to Charles, was more ambivalent. Although Dickens didn't forbid intercourse between the children and their mother, she was well aware of how he disliked it when they saw her. (She told Gladys Storey that for almost two years after the separation, her father "would scarcely speak to [her] because she visited her mother.") Yet Katey took the easy path, not quarreling with her father's legal rights and more or less distancing herself from Catherine, although unlike Mamie she was sensitive to this disloyalty, and later would regret it deeply: "We were *all* very wicked" not to side with "my poor, poor mother."

We have also seen how this disruption of the family affected the way the girls were viewed and judged in mid-

Victorian society. Why weren't they with their mother? What was Georgina's role in the family drama? It was all a tremendous scandal, and Katey's life became increasingly wretched, almost desperate, all the more so because Dickens was in a frenzy of anger, pugnacity, self-righteousness, self-pity, and self-justification. "My father was like a madman when my mother left home," Katey would one day acknowledge. And of his liaison with Ellen Ternan, "This affair brought out all that was worst—all that was weakest in him. He did not care a damn what happened to any of us. Nothing could surpass the misery and unhappiness of our home."

However much the Dickens children loved their father, they were also afraid of him, and besides, what could they do? Mamie accepted the new situation without hesitation or remorse. Charley was more or less on his own. The other boys were all being prepared to be shed. What Katey did was the only thing possible for a young woman whose domestic situation had become unbearable: She decided to marry.

There had been a number of men attracted to her—she was pretty, bright, and the daughter of Charles Dickens—but she could not have Edmund Yates, and no one else particularly interested her. On the edge of the family circle, however, was Charlie Collins,* Wilkie's younger brother, an admired artist and a personable young man. He had always been drawn to Katey, and now, when he proposed late in 1859, she accepted him.

No one thought it was a very good idea. Dickens, of

---

*To help the reader keep track: "Charles" is Dickens himself; "Charley" is his oldest child, Katey's big brother; "Charlie" is the man she marries.

course, believed that no one was worthy enough for his be-loved daughter, and beyond that, Charlie Collins was gener-ally considered to be something of an odd one. He had gone through a highly ascetic period, denying himself his pre-ferred foods (like his favorite blackberry tart) and refusing to dance although he was very good at it and enjoyed it. He was nice-looking—according to his friend the artist William Holman Hunt, "slight, with slender limbs, but erect in the head and shoulders, beautifully cut features, large chin, a crop of orange-coloured hair (latterly a beard), blue eyes that look at a challenger without a sign of quailing." He was gentle, ami-able, and, having passed thirty, had reached the age when he felt he should settle down. (Wilkie told his and Charlie's beloved mother that "Charlie is still trying hard to talk him-self into believing that he ought to be married.") Most of all, he was sympathetic. Katey later acknowledged that she was not in the least in love with him, but that she "considered him the kindest and most sweet-tempered of men."

Also, they were both artists and they shared artist friends, particularly John Everett Millais, whose fame was at its height. During the time of their engagement, Millais asked Dickens's permission, which was granted, to use Katey as a model for what would be one of his most famous pictures, *The Black Brunswicker*, depicting a pretty English girl clinging to her fiancé, a Prussian soldier, as he is departing for Water-loo. Katey obeyed the conventions of the time: She could pose in Millais's studio only with a chaperone present, and she not only couldn't be painted clinging to a man—the two figures were painted separately—but the two models never even met.

The preparations for the wedding in midsummer 1860 were almost oddly rushed, and although a special train was brought

Katey as the young woman in Millais's The Black Brunswicker

down to Gad's Hill from London to accommodate the guests, and there were appropriate decorations and sumptuous food, the wedding day was somewhat muted. Dickens was obviously unhappy about the marriage, Mamie was in tears, and Katey was far from an ecstatic bride. No one could fail to notice the absence of the bride's mother; Charles had forbidden her to attend. (It's difficult to understand how Katey could have been complicit with this cruelty.) After Katey and Charlie left for their wedding tour on the Continent and all the guests had departed, the dejected Dickens was left alone with Georgina and Mamie, who later reported that, going up to her sister's bedroom and opening the door, "she beheld her father upon his knees with his head buried in Katie's wedding gown, sobbing. She stood for some moments before he became aware of her presence; when at last he got up and saw her, he said in a broken voice: 'But for me, Katie would not have left home,' and walked out of the room."

The newlyweds decided to stay in Europe for some time. Money was one reason: Dickens had been generous with Katey's dowry, but Charlie Collins had stopped painting— talented as he was, he felt he could not achieve the perfection he aspired to; as the son of the famous landscape and genre artist William Collins and the close friend of such luminaries as Millais and Hunt and the other early Pre-Raphaelites, he no doubt felt intimidated. Now he was earning his living as a writer, his father-in-law having hired him to contribute to *All the Year Round*, and he was planning a book based on his and Katey's wanderings in Europe.

Both he and Katey had always lived in comfort; now they were relatively poor, and Charlie had always been anxious about money and reluctant to spend it—his letters to his mother are filled with reports of how cheaply they were living, first in Calais, then in Paris. It's clear that they were enjoying being on their own, and they were finding that they were good companions. Katey enjoyed describing to Harriet Collins, her much-loved mother-in-law, their domestic contentment. "We cook our own food, no one in the world could cook a chop better than Charlie does, and I am very great indeed at boiled rice. In the morning Charlie lights the fire and I lay the cloth, while he fries the bacon I make the tea. After breakfast I clear away, put his writing materials out on the table and he sets down to work while I wash up the breakfast cups in the kitchen, put away everything, sweep up the crumbs and the hearth and get the room neat."

But although the young couple may have been good companions, it appears that they did not have a satisfactory sexual relationship—if they had one at all. The consensus is that their marriage was never consummated. Katey was to tell her mother-in-law that she and Charlie slept in separate beds, and her father that "Charles ought never to have married." Frederick Lehmann, in no way a malicious observer, was to write that Charlie's getting married was "an infamy." There is supposition about his being homosexual, perhaps not in practice but in inclination, and he may have married to escape those tendencies. Certainly Katey never became pregnant by him. Yet the marriage at this point cannot be called an unhappy one. Away from her family, Katey was recovering from the misery she had fled, and she and Charlie had great affection for each other and trusted each other.

They were abroad for half a year—in Paris, Lausanne, Brussels, on the road. When they returned to London in early 1861, they stayed first with Mrs. Collins, then in a small flat of their own in Kensington, a neighborhood where many of their artist friends lived. Apparently, Katey had ignored her art while abroad, but now she went back to it seriously and began to have some success, particularly as a portraitist. She and Charlie were spending a good deal of time at Gad's Hill, and were caught up in a social world that included not only artists like Millais and Holman Hunt but the formidable Lord

Frederic Leighton. Closest of all was the Thackeray family. Not only had the Dickens and Thackeray girls been frequently together from childhood on, but Charlie Collins had grown very close to Thackeray himself, despite the disparity in their ages. Katey, in fact, was instrumental in healing a painful breach between Thackeray and her father that had resulted from a foolish disagreement years earlier. Stubborn, proud Dickens could not apologize or accept blame, but when Thackeray asked Katey whether her father would reciprocate if he made the first move, she told him she was certain he would. Later, she wrote about what happened in *Pall Mall* magazine:

> Thackeray . . . came to our house with radiant face to tell me the result. "How did it happen?" said I. "Oh," he said gaily, "your father knew he was wrong and was full of apologies—" It was now my turn to look severe. "You know you are not telling me the truth, you wicked man. Please let me hear immediately what really did happen." Thackeray's eyes were very kind as he said quite simply, "I met him at the Athenaeum Club and held out my hand, saying we had been foolish long enough—or words to that effect; your father grasped it very cordially—and—we are friends again, thank God!

When Thackeray died not long afterward, not only did Dickens write a magnificent tribute to him, but Thackeray's mother and his girls came at once to stay with Katey and Charlie until after the funeral.

The second half of the 1860s was a period of stress, unhappiness, and illness for both the Collinses. Charlie had always been physically weak, and now he was in constant pain, and on several occasions apparently close to death; the pain was so severe that he couldn't sit up to paint or draw—Dickens had commissioned him to do the illustrations for *Edwin Drood* but he gave up after only one week. In 1867, Dickens wrote to an American friend, "Charley Collins is—*I* say emphatically—dying. Only last night I thought it was all over. He is reduced to that state of weakness, and is so racked and worn by a horrible strange vomiting, that if he were to faint— as he must at last—I do not think he could be revived." He was angry with this useless son-in-law. Dickens could not, Fechter told Annie Fields, "understand the prolonged endurance of such an existence and in his passionate nature which must snap when it yielded at all, it produced disgust." Yet in the event, Charlie would outlive his father-in-law, if not for long.

No one could provide an accurate diagnosis of Charlie's illness, and in the mid-sixties he and Katey tried various spas in Europe, warm climates, new medications, without any prolonged improvement. During this time, Katey, as physically fragile as ever, exhausted herself and made herself seriously ill in nursing him. Anny Thackeray was to write in her memoirs of remembering how once, when his daughter was laid up in bed with a dangerous fever, Dickens told her "that in those miserable days his very coming seemed to bring healing and peace to her as she lay, and to quiet the raging fever. He knew how critical the illness was, but he spoke quietly and with good courage." As in her childhood, only her father could soothe Katey when she was ill.

When she was well, her impulsive and provocative behavior caused unfortunate comment in society. In 1866, Lehmann reports to his wife after a dinner party that "Kitty looked a spectacle of woe . . . and was quite distracted . . .

When she smiled something of her former pretty self reappeared, only to make the pained and woebegone expression that would follow more distressing." By the late sixties, the Lehmanns' letters are suggesting that Katey was "intensely eager . . . to find other lovers." This would hardly be surprising considering that it is likely that after almost a decade of marriage she was still a virgin.

Various men have been suggested as lovers of hers at this time, but the most likely was the robust, virile Valentine Prinsep, who not only was a talented artist but was connected to many of the leading artistic and literary figures of the time, the Tennysons and the Thackerays among them. He had been taught by the renowned G. F. Watts and encouraged by Dante Gabriel Rossetti. (Anny Thackeray reported visiting the Prinsep family in their summer home on the Isle of Wight, where "Everybody is either a genius, or a poet, or a painter or peculiar in some way.") It was believed at the time that Prinsep was very much in love with Katey, and in 1925, Lady Lucy Mathews, a lifelong friend of Katey's, revealed that Katey had indeed been so "deeply in love with Val Prinsep that it made her very ill." Prinsep, a man strongly attracted to women and attractive to them as well, did not marry until 1884, when he was in his forties and Katey had remarried.

Katey's emotional difficulties may have been assuaged by her liaison with Prinsep, but she and Charlie were struggling financially. He could no longer work, and her painting was not yet remunerative enough to sustain them. Her father, generous to her as always, supplemented her income, but with Charlie increasingly debilitated and in need of constant attention, the Collinses were living on the edge—one reason, surely, that they so frequently stayed at Gad's Hill, with all its comforts, and where Mamie and Georgina could help with Charlie. By now it had been discovered that he was suffering from an incurable cancer of the stomach. Even so, they lived a life of pleasant surfaces. In 1869, Annie Fields, on a visit from Boston, described Katey as being "like a piece of old china with a picture by Sir Joshua Reynolds painted upon it and with manners as piquant peculiar and taking as such a painting come to life ought to have . . . Although the effect is like some rare strange thing, which does not quite wear away in spite of her piquancy; for she is clever enough to be a match for the best of us I am sure." She also very much admired the Collinses' artistic home. Katey had very little money, she explained, but preferred "the deprivations poverty brings to receiving from her father or allowing her husband who is very ill to overwork himself." Most telling: Katey very much resembled her father, "especially in her indomitable reserve of temper equal to any emergency."

Early in 1870, Katey and Mamie were participating in a number of private theatricals, and Katey's acting was much admired. Charles, in increasingly bad health, actually came to watch his girls perform, though he kept himself out of view. Soon after that, a professional actor-manager offered Katey a contract as an actress, and on June 4 she went to Gad's Hill to discuss the possibility with her father. "You are pretty and no doubt would do well, but you are too sensitive a nature to bear the brunt of much you would encounter. Although there are nice people on the stage, there are some who would make your hair stand on end. You are clever enough to do something else." (Years later, she told George Bernard Shaw, "I took it to my father, but he was more severe on the subject of the profession than you are. I had to refuse it to my sorrow.") He did, however, approve of her painting, having several months earlier written to his intimate friend William Macready, the nation's leading tragedian and Katey's godfather, "Katie has made some more capital portraits and is always improving." Dickens was knowledgeable about art; his approval was worth having. Millais also, Georgina had informed Annie, had been highly positive about Katey's work, giving her "the strongest encouragement to persevere—which delighted her very much and pleased her Father too."

The conversation on the night of June 4 was very long and very intimate. Dickens, Katey was to say, had spoken to her of things he had always previously hidden: about his child-hood? about Ellen Ternan? "I shall never forget that talk," she told Gladys Storey, the great confidante of her later years. He spoke of his regrets: "He wished, he said, he had been 'a better father, a better man,'" and she added, "He was not a good man, but he was not a fast man, but he was wonderful! He fell in love with this girl, I did not blame *her*—it is never one person's fault."

The next morning, as she was about to set off for the train back to London, she had an irresistible impulse to see her father again and walked through the tunnel that led under the road separating the main house from the miniature cha-let where Dickens wrote every morning. "His head was bent low down over his work, and he turned an eager and rather flushed face towards me as I entered. On ordinary occasions he would just have raised his cheek for my kiss, saying a few words, perhaps . . . but on this morning, when he saw me he pushed his chair from the writing-table, opened his arms, and took me into them," saying "God bless you, Katie." When she was halfway through the tunnel returning to the house, "something said to me, 'go back,' and I immediately ran up the steps, through the shrubbery, into the Châlet and tapped on the door. My father—who was seated with his back to it—called out, 'Come in'; turning and seeing me he held out his arms into which I ran, when he embraced me again and kissed me very affectionately." It was later that day that he suffered his fatal stroke, and by the time Katey and Mamie could rush back from London, he was in the coma from which he never woke.

These final encounters between father and daughter confirm—if we require confirmation—the powerful love and understanding that bound them together. More than thirty-five years later Katey would write about their last long conversation: "He spoke as if his life were over and there was nothing left. And so we sat on, he talking, and I only interrupting him now and then to give him a word of sympathy and love. The early summer dawn was creeping into the conservatory before we went upstairs together and I left him at his bedroom door. But I could not forget his words and sleep was impossible." We must be grateful that they had these last hours together.

WALTER

Walter Savage Landor Dickens, 1841–1863

WALTER DICKENS—Charles and Catherine's fourth child in five years—was the first of them to be named after a renowned literary figure, the distinguished poet, epigrammatist, and author of the celebrated *Imaginary Conversations*, a cantankerous, litigious, and widely loved man.

Little Walter would have had to be a prodigious child to live up to this eminence, and although he had wholesome and charming qualities, literary genius was not one of them. (As a child he enjoyed writing, but his father discouraged him from continuing at it—probably aware, writes Lucinda Hawksley, "that he did not have the aptitude or ambition to work at [it] as hard as he would need to do in order to succeed financially.") As with the other children, Dickens was both proud of and comically rueful at this latest arrival. "All I know is that he has large dark eyes, and no nose at all as yet—except that he seems to live in a state of perpetual sleepiness and intoxication (except when he cries)—is very fat—and looks when he is being washed, like a plucked turkey." In

Walter Dickens in uniform, 1857

other words, with his relentless eye and pen, Dickens turned his child into a Dickens character. As an infant he was nicknamed "Young Skull," for his high cheekbones.

Apparently, he was a good-natured, accommodating little boy. By the time he was eight, Dickens was fretting about his future, consulting, naturally, with Coutts, who was prepared to do something for him. But what? Dickens didn't believe Walter was clever enough to follow Charley to Eton. Her idea was that she would sponsor him for an East India Company cadetship—that is, a military life. (She was a major shareholder in the company.) Dickens describes Walter, at nine, as "a tougher subject than Charley, not so quick or sensitive, a hard-working, patient, capable child, better fitted in all respects for such a life, and much more safely to be left to himself. I feel certain he would strive on and do well in India." So Walter's life was disposed of.

When he's ten, he's sent to a Mr. Trimmer in Putney who "educates expressly for India. I don't think he is so clever as Charley," Dickens repeats to Coutts, "but he is a very steady amiable boy, of a good reliable capacity, and brings exalted certificates from Mr. King" (his current schoolmaster). When he's twelve, Dickens writes to Landor, the boy's god-father, "Walter is a very good boy, and comes home from school with honourable commendation. He passed last Sunday in solitary confinement (in a bathroom) on bread and water, for terminating a dispute with the nurse by throwing a chair in her direction. It is the very first occasion of his ever having got into trouble, for he is a great favourite with the whole house, and one of the most amiable boys in the boy world. (He comes out on birthdays in a blaze of shirt pin.)" The shirt pin had been a gift from Landor. Dickens reports that Walter, as he headed back to school, "departed from the parental roof, with a plum cake, a box of marmalade, a ditto of jam, twelve oranges, five shillings, and a gross of tears."

At this distance, and from the scant evidence, Walter sounds like a normal, decent, energetic lad. Perhaps too energetic for his father, who when the boys are all home from school complains of their feet stomping up and down the stairs, with Walter, at fourteen, the loudest of all. "Why a boy of that age should seem to have on at all times, 150 pairs of double soled boots, and to be always jumping a bottom stair with the whole 150, I don't know." Perhaps such irritations contributed to Dickens's far from reluctant view, as expressed to Coutts in a letter of October, 1856: "I have no doubt that it will be best for Walter to go out at once. I believe it will be far better for his health, and certainly for his spirits, and no less for his duties. The staying with his brothers and sisters with that unsettled purpose on him and cloud of departure hanging over him, would do him no good and would be (I much suspect from what I see of him) a kind of cruelty."

He wouldn't be at home for long. By the time he reached fifteen, he had done well enough at school to be ready to take the arduous exams for his East India cadetship in only a year, and in April 1857, Dickens reported to Coutts:

> You will be glad to hear that Walter appeared here yesterday, radiant and gleaming. He passed his examination on Tuesday in a most creditable manner, and was one of a small number of boys out of a large number, who emerged from the Ordeal triumphant. I have now taken order [*sic*] for his learning to swim, to ride, to fence, to become acquainted with the use of gun and pistol, and to "go in" for a trifle of Hindustanee, in the course of the three months he will probably remain at home . . . He was perfectly happy . . . and he was very anxious I should "tell Miss Coutts that he hadn't been spun"—which means, rejected.

Soon after, Dickens wrote to Coutts that Walter, having a direct appointment to the East India Company through her influence, will probably "be sent out soon" and so "will fall into that strange life 'up the country' before he well knows that he is alive, or what life is—which indeed seems to be rather an advanced state of knowledge."

On July 20, 1857, the sixteen-year-old Walter sailed for India aboard the *Indus*. Apparently, he wept at the separation from his mother and the girls and the younger boys, and his father and Charley went down to Southampton with him to see him off. Dickens, of course, was distressed, but as Peter Ackroyd writes, "there is no evidence to suggest that [he] was particularly upset about Walter's departure for Walter's own sake; his lament is generalized." "I left the poor fellow on board the Indus yesterday," he wrote to a friend, "in good spirits—as little cast down as, at 16, one could reasonably hope to be with the world of India before one." On board, Walter had run into an old school friend, and the ship's captain had assured Dickens that Walter would be well looked after.

It is unlikely that either father or son was aware that only weeks earlier, an uprising in India—the menacing "Indian Mutiny," or "Sepoy Rebellion"—had broken out; it was not until a week after Walter had sailed that Disraeli informed the House of Commons of what was happening on the subcontinent. By then, the famous siege of Lucknow was already in place, and the town of Kanpur had been captured, its entire European population slaughtered.*

Walter arrived in Calcutta on August 30, was soon assigned to Her Majesty's 42nd Highlanders (the Black Watch), and was quickly embroiled, as his father put it, "in the thick of the tussle," actively involved in the relief of Lucknow and other important engagements. In December, Dickens wrote that he didn't exactly know where Walter was, but "He liked

---

*For most of my information in this section, I have relied on an article called "The Short Career of Walter Dickens in India" by Dick Kooiman, published in 2002 in *The Dickensian*.

the country and the life, of all things, and is quite happy." A year later he is encouraging the mother of another Indian cadet:

My boy was invalided long ago, and carried in a litter God knows how far and how long. But he began to get well, the moment he arrived at a Hill-Station, and his only care now, in the letters he writes home, is to get away from that easy life and be on service again. He had sun-stroke, a passing-attack of small pox, and smart Fever. But he rallied, gaily—and so will your boy."

Kooiman writes:

Maybe, the cheerful tone of what we know of Walter's letters should be explained by a light-heartedness of youth and the fact that the confusion during the Mutiny had enabled him to gain rapid promotion in the army. He had gone out as an Ensign, but already before the age of 18 he was made a Lieutenant in the thinned ranks of the Queen's 42nd Highlanders; and he "got a lot of prize-money besides." What certainly also must have contributed to his feeling of contentment was the military honours, a "Mutiny medal with clasp," which he received for his part in the operations of H.M.s 42nd Royal Highlanders against Lucknow and in the field in the North-Western Provinces.

But if in these early days Walter was proving himself (and being rewarded) on the battlefield, he was already falling into severe financial difficulties—by the time he was nineteen he was piling up debts, damaging his position within his regiment (he was placed low on the list for a captainship), and angering his father. When Charley, on his tea-purchasing trip to the Far East, spent a fortnight with Walter in October 1861, he paid his outstanding bills for him, but soon there were new ones. Dickens sent him more than £100 in that same year, reporting to a friend, "My second boy with the 42nd Highlanders in India, spends more than he gets and has cost me money and disappointed me." Finally, he called a halt, sternly pointing out to Walter that he had bailed him out too often and that, although he was very sorry, and not angry, "he must now, as a matter of common reason and justice to his other brothers, live upon his own means." At this rebuke, Walter stopped writing home, except once, to Mamie, stating that he wouldn't be back in touch until he was out of debt. He had earlier considered asking for a transfer to home service, but this would have involved reducing his income, and Dickens had advised against it.

We know almost nothing of Walter's personal life in India—whether his money was being spent on women or elegant clothes or, as is most likely, on gambling. But his situation had become desperate, and his health was collapsing as well. Finally he wrote again to Mamie telling her that he was ill, and months after that another letter arrived saying that he was being sent home on sick leave. He was, he told her, "so weak that he could hardly crawl." The family was expecting him at Gad's Hill.

On February 7, 1864—Dickens's birthday—a telegram arrived from the officers' hospital in Calcutta: "It is my most painful duty to inform you of the sudden death of your son Lieut. Walter Landor Dickens." Dickens narrates the circumstances in a letter to Coutts:

He arrived at Calcutta, from the Station where his regiment was, on the 27th. of December. He was consigned by the Regimental Doctor to the Officers' Hospital there, which is a very fine place. On the last day of the old year at a quarter past 5 in the afternoon he was talking to the other patients about his arrangements for coming home, when he became excited, coughed violently, had a great gush of blood from the mouth, and fell dead;—all this, in a few seconds. It was then found that there was extensive and perfectly incurable aneurism of the Aorta, which had burst. I could have wished it had pleased God to let him see his home again; but I think he would have died at the door.

The immediate cause of his death, his sisters and Charley and I, keep to ourselves; both because his Aunt [Georgina] has the same disorder, and because we observe strong traces of it in one of his brothers [in all likelihood, Sydney].

Katey would write to Anny Thackeray that Mamie "felt dear Wally's death very much—I don't believe he is dead—I feel he must be coming home. Oh, I think he might have been allowed to live just to see home once more." As for Catherine, Sir William Hardman, editor of the *Morning Post*, wrote, "Poor Mrs. Charles Dickens is in great grief at the loss of the second son, Walter Landor Dickens, who has died with his regiment in India . . . her grief is much enhanced by the fact that her husband has not taken any notice of the event to her, either by letter or otherwise. If anything were wanting to sink Charles Dickens to the lowest depths of my esteem, this fills up the measure of his iniquity. As a writer, I admire him; as a man, I despise him." Hardman would have been further incensed if he had known that the inscription on Walter's tombstone, in Calcutta, reads: "In memory of Lieut. Walter Landor Dickens, The second son of Charles Dickens, who died at the Officers' Hospital, Calcutta, On his way home on sick leave, December 31st, 1863, Aged 23." Apparently, Walter had no mother. Nor was he yet twenty-three.

A few months after the news of Walter's death came a letter from his commanding officer enclosing an assortment of unpaid bills: "I feel I could not do my duty if I withheld these from you," he wrote, adding, "Let me take this opportunity of saying that the death of your son caused us all sincere sorrow; for he was a favourite with us all; and not all his difficulties in pecuniary matters, which appear to have begun immediately after he came to India, affected or in any way diminished our regard for him." It rings true—the amiable and modest Walter had always been "a favourite."

His personal possessions at his death were pathetically meager: a small trunk, changes of linen, some prayer books, and a photograph of a woman, presumably a recent one of Georgina. Apparently, he had sold everything else to help pay for his trip home. The outstanding bills, spelled out in Arthur Adrian's biography of Georgina, included ones from the officers' mess, the regimental store, the billiard table, and a merchant or two—the total, apart from servants' wages, came to more than £100. A final appeal for restitution came from an Indian creditor:

Humble petition of Gunga Rum Cloth
    Most humbly sheweth
    I most humbly beg to write these few humble lines
to your greate honour

—Honoured Sir—

Your poor petitioner is want 14 Re 8 ans. [fourteen rupees and eight annas] from April 1862 and he havent payed to me yet and Sir

I have heard now Dickens is gone to England some days ago and Sir now I will get these Re with your kind

Should I be so fortunate as to succeed my request for which act of generosity I shall ever pray for your long life and prosperity.

History does not relate whether this petition was successful.

Just short of a month after receiving the news of Walter's death, Dickens wrote to the Reverend T. W. Gyldhawk, "A poor boy whom you Christened died in India, a grown man, on the last day of this last old year. All my other sons are well and working their various ways." (This, alas, proved to be a false assessment.)

As for Walter, he had, as Dickens made known, been a disappointment. And a bewilderment. How to account for this normal, passive, likable boy? On the day the sixteen-year-old Walter sailed for India—long before the debts and the tragedy of his early death—Dickens wrote to a friend, "I don't at all know this day how he comes to be mine, or I his."

Walter, on the other hand, knew exactly who his father was. When filling out the official application for joining the East India Company, he answered the automatic question "What is the profession, situation, and residence of your Parents or nearest of Kin" with the simple answer: "My father Charles Dickens Esq., Tavistock House." That was all anyone needed to be told; it was the defining reality for every one of the children.

FRANK

Francis Jeffrey Dickens, 1844–1886

FRANK DICKENS was a problem when he was alive, and he's still a problem today. What to make of him? The fifth Dickens child and the third son, he didn't, and doesn't, make much of an impression, except that of a disappointing and disappointed, if well-meaning, boy and man. Dickens, not yet thirty-two, announces his birth with less than his habitual enthusiasm: "Nurses, wet and dry; apothecaries; mothers-in-laws [*sic*]; babies; with all the sweet (and chaste) delights of private life." Just eight months earlier he had written to a friend whose wife had recently given birth, "I hope *my* missis won't do so never no more." In a letter a month after the birth, he remarks, "Kate is all right again, and so . . . is the Baby. But I decline (on principle) to look at the latter object." (Presumably, the reference to Kate's [Catherine's] being "all right again" means that the obligatory "chaste" period is behind him.)

Even the origin of Frank's nickname—"Chickenstalker"—is in doubt. One source claims it's descriptive of "his make-believe hunting adventures around the home place." More

Frank Dickens

generally, it's ascribed to a character in "The Chimes," the long, sentimental, and hugely popular Christmas story Dickens had published just before Frank was born. Peter Ackroyd comments, "The fact that Francis was named after a character in 'The Chimes' suggests how easily Dickens moved from his fictional family to his real family." But why would you name a baby boy after a jolly, fat old lady? Was baby Frank conspicuously jolly and fat? If so, we have no record of it.

There are early positive mentions of him. As a baby, Dickens writes, he's "decidedly a success—a perpetual grin is on his face: and the spoon exercise is amazing." Writing to Catherine, he reports the six-year-old Frank as being "so handsome that he is quite a sight to behold." He was thought by some to be most like Charles "in face, gesture and manner," and at one point his father refers to him as "the cleverest of all the children"—this, in connection to the discovery by Dickens "to my great vexation and distress, this morning, that they have kept [from] me that Frank . . . stammers so horribly as to be quite an afflicted object." But how could Dickens, who spent so much time with his children, not have noticed this affliction in a boy who lived at home? Did Catherine manage to hide it from him, and if so, why?

Typically, Dickens set about trying to cure his son, but when did all this happen? One account—and common sense—suggests that Frank was six or seven when the discovery was made, not long before he was sent off to school in Boulogne, where Charley and Walter had preceded him, and where the headmaster was instructed by Dickens to give him a daily glass of "porter" to help build up the boy's strength. Yet Alfred Dickens, Frank's junior by two years, would one day write that in the summer of 1859 Dickens was racing to finish *A Tale of Two Cities* "with tremendous interest and fervour," and though "working night and day at very high pressure, used to have Frank in his study every morning. He would read him a passage of Shakespeare and then would make my brother Frank do the same thing, over and over again, very slowly and distinctly. Finally my father made a complete cure of him."

There are several difficulties with this account. Frank in 1859 was already fifteen, and in Germany to learn the language in preparation for becoming a doctor, an early, unrealistic ambition. (Could Alfred have conflated *A Tale of Two Cities* with an earlier novel? *David Copperfield* would be the most likely candidate.) And, alas, Frank's stammer was *never* completely cured. (He was also a sleepwalker.)

The German experiment began in the inevitable confusion that seemed to dog the young Frank. In September 1858, Dickens wrote to a friend that the boy had been sent by steamer to Hamburg. A letter from the traveler duly arrived, with what Dickens called an "astonishing postscript" explaining that no one met him at the dock, that the other passengers had long since left the ship, and that he was staying on board dining with the captain and mate on beefsteak and onions. ("It is very good, and there is lots of it.") "My own impression," wrote Dickens, "is, that he will sail backwards and forwards in the John Bull, like a Young Flying Dutchman, for many years, and will vainly try, until he arrives at a green old age, to get to school."

When the German experience fizzled out—Frank was not meant for medicine *or* German—Dickens had him doing some work at the *All the Year Round* offices, but that experiment fizzled out, too. Ditto a plan for him to enter into business with Charley. At one point, Frank announced that he might like to be a gentleman farmer: Give him a horse, a rifle, and a stake of fifteen pounds, and he thought he could end up "very comfortable." His father thought differently: "I perceived that the first consequence of the fifteen pounds would be that he would be robbed of it, of the horse that it would throw him, and of the rifle that it would blow his head off." Hardly a vote of confidence.

Finally, Dickens procured Frank an appointment to the Bengal Mounted Police and dispatched him to India, where he arrived not long after Walter had died but before that news had reached England. He was just twenty, and he would be six years into his apparently satisfactory career there, about which we know no particulars, when his father died. As had been the case with Walter, and later would be the case with Alfred and Plorn, Frank and his father would never see each other again after he left England. "A good steady fellow," was Dickens's verdict on him, "but not at all brilliant."

ALFRED

Alfred d'Orsay Tennyson Dickens, 1845–1912

KATE CONFINED, thank God, at half past ten this morning with what is usually called (I don't know why) a chopping boy. I am partial to girls, and had set my heart on one—but never mind me." So Dickens to his friend Clarkson Stanfield, on October 28, 1845. And about nine months later, to one of the boy's godfathers, the dashing and brilliantly accomplished man-about-Europe Alfred, Count d'Orsay (on whom, by the way, *The New Yorker*'s Eustace Tilley was modeled), "Your Godson's Mama and Nurses are, and have been ever since we left home, so desperately importunate to have a Report made to you—a true and ungarnished report of his unparalleled and never-sufficiently-to-be-wondered-at-Goodness—that I must, for the sake of peace and quietness, begin my letter with it. So pray take notice that he is never known to cry; that he came through the long journey [to Switzerland] and great heat without the slightest remonstrance of any sort or kind; that he is perpetually laughing and good tempered; and I see him at this moment lying in the Garden, in the shade, with his two pink legs upreared in the air, and *the* bells and Coral forced into his mouth." (The bells and Coral clearly a godfatherly gift from d'Orsay.)

A happy baby then, and good-tempered. He began as he meant to go on: Sixty-seven years later, at his death, he is again and again referred to as "kindly." Which doesn't explain why his nickname was "Skittles." Nor why with two godfathers named Alfred, his own Uncle Alfred, a younger brother of Dickens's of whom the novelist was always fond, was left out of the equation.

Alfred was the fourth of Dickens's sons, with three to follow—he was right in the middle, and seems not to have had a special place in the family: neither the oldest nor the youngest; not particularly clever or enchanting, like Sydney, but not troubled, like Frank; not the solid achiever like Harry nor the beloved but somewhat dim Benjamin of the family: that was Plorn.

He seems to have had a normal childhood—or as normal as a Dickens child could have. (Not every little boy of seven is wakened at 3:00 a.m. to be taken down to the offices of *Household Words* to await the funeral procession of the great Duke of Wellington.) He was subject, like all his siblings, to the strictures on neatness and order that Dickens imposed on his entire family. "I was busily engaged brushing my coat in the dining-room instead of outside," Alfred wrote decades later. "He happened to come in at that moment and I never by any chance committed that particular offence afterwards." But, he added, "If ever he did allow his temper to get the better of him for a few moments, which however he rarely did, then like the sun after a passing shadow, all the most lovable traits of his most lovable character shone out to greater advantage afterwards." Like Charley, he wrote with nostalgia and affection of outings with his father, reporting on snipe-shooting in "those very Essex Marshes" that feature in *Great Expectations*. He also recounted how he and his brothers used to row their father from "Rochester to Maidstone, when he used to act as coxswain and laugh and chaff us all the time . . . He was a splendid companion for children . . ." with a "very droll mind and a very humorous way of putting things." (So the entire world had already discovered.)

Alfred clearly had spirit. When he was three, Dickens writes (in French) to d'Orsay: "He's a good boy—very strong and proud." And two years later—the boy is now five—"Your godson sends his respects. He's savage and ferocious—not yet civilized." Dickens was later to describe him as "a remarkable character as a combination of self-reliance, steadiness, and adventurous spirit—whom I have always purposed to send abroad, and whom I believe to be particularly qualified for this opportunity." He was sent, as were Frank, Sydney, and Harry—to school in Boulogne to perfect his French, and the idea was that he would follow Walter to the Wimbledon School, to prepare for the entrance exams for the army. Alas, he failed his exams, and there arose the question Dickens had to face seven times with his seven boys: What to do with him? There was a brief notion of a career in medicine, then he decided on commerce, and his father found a place for him with a firm doing business with the Far East. It did not work out.

But Alfred liked the idea of going overseas, and the idea of emigration began to emerge. Dickens had long been interested in Australia—there are frequent articles about it in his magazine—and of course it was to Australia that the Micawbers repaired at the end of *David Copperfield*, and from which the convict Magwitch escapes in *Great Expectations*. Oddly enough, it was also to Australia that Anthony Trollope's son Frederic migrated in 1863, and the sons of the two famous novelists would find themselves living in the same area of the outback. The senior Trollopes would visit their son in Australia; Dickens never did, although he twice weighed touring there.

Dickens threw himself into his typical practice of making connections for his boys—writing or calling on distinguished and/or successful men who could introduce the newly arrived emigrant to other potentially useful connections, and could also be fallback authorities or safeguards should things go wrong. And because Dickens was Dickens, everyone was happy to accommodate him. On the other hand, Alfred, like his brother Plorn after him, had no immediate situation to enter into in Australia; he had to make his own way, like Dick Whittington—except for the introductions and, of course, the Dickens name.

To his friend Austen Layard, a famous archaeologist as well as undersecretary for foreign affairs, Dickens wrote of Alfred:

He is twenty years of age, and unmarried. He has been for two years and more, in a large China House in the City and has a special aptitude for business, and a sound practical knowledge of it. His object is, to become employed in some business-house in the new world . . . No arrangements are made for him (beyond providing him with introductions) and as he is going out of his own

Alfred Dickens as a young dandy

desire—as the storybooks say, "to seek his fortune." I believe him to have a knowledge and habit of business, not by any means common in well educated youths of his age.

There was no mention of Alfred's having become something of a dandy (like his father at the same age) and, like several of his brothers, in debt—for such purchases as eleven pairs of kid gloves, eight silk scarves, three pairs of trousers, a treble-milled coat and vest (whatever "treble-milled" may be), as well as handkerchiefs, cameo and onyx scarf pins, a traveling rug, two umbrellas, a silver-mounted cane, and a bottle of scent and eight pairs of ladies' gloves. The assumption is that these last items were meant as presents for his mother, sisters, and Georgina. Alfred was always generous.

Layard responded warmly and Dickens was soon effusively thanking him for "letters on my son's behalf. As to a letter from the Colonial Office to the Governor, presenting him as my son, I should be very glad to have it, if you can without laying yourself under obligation or putting yourself to inconvenience obtain it in the course of the week."

Central to Alfred's eventual life in Australia was an introduction to George Rusden, about whom one Australian historian wrote, "By the time he was thirty, there was not an aspect of the pastoral industry he did not know, hardly a squatter in Southern New South Wales whose acquaintance he had not made." Almost ten years before Alfred arrived in Melbourne, Rusden had become Clerk of Parliaments when the colony achieved self-government; he was also a leading cultural force, a writer, poet, and Shakespeare scholar. From the start he was a staunch friend to both Alfred and Plorn, and a source of both information and comfort to Dickens. "Again I have to thank you very heartily for your kindness in writing to me about my son. The intelligence you send me concerning him is a great relief and satisfaction to my mind and I cannot separate these feelings from a truly grateful recognition of the advice and assistance for which he is much beholden to you or from his strong desire to deserve of your good opinion. Believe me always my Dear Sir. Your faithful and truly obliged Charles Dickens." Rusden would remain a faithful friend to both young men until he retired to England in 1882, and a faithful and warm correspondent of Dickens's until the latter's death.

His reports on Alfred were generous and positive. It isn't possible to trace the young man's first actions after reaching Melbourne in December 1865, but he seems to have fared well from the start, and within a year had taken up a job as manager of a sheep station called Conoble, well north of Melbourne in New South Wales. Clearly, he took to the life, very much enjoying his new situation; Dickens writes to Rusden in 1867, "He describes himself as being 'as happy as a king' and his interest in his occupation seems inseparable from a wholesome sense of responsibility."

By the following year, he had moved on to a presumably more satisfying job as manager of another sheep station, Corona, in the recently explored Darling River Barrier Ranges, where Rusden reports to Dickens "he has displayed resolution enough to apply himself . . . it requires resolution for a young man who has moved in good society to apply himself to the details of bush life. That resolution your son Alfred has shown."

How gratifying this must have been to Dickens after his disappointments over his older sons. In his final letter to Alfred, written only weeks before his death in 1870, he wrote that he had had "the best accounts" of him from an Australian visitor to England. "I told him," wrote Dickens, "that they did not surprise me, for I had unbounded faith in you. For which take my love and blessing. This is not a letter so much as an assurance that I never think of you without hope and comfort." This letter reached Alfred after Dickens had died, and must to some degree have eased his grief. Not often had one of Dickens's sons received so forthright a signal of his father's approval.

SYDNEY

Sydney Smith Haldimand Dickens, 1847–1872

WHEREAS DICKENS never seemed to have a particular interest in Walter or Frank, little Sydney charmed and fascinated him from the very first. (When Sydney was four, his father referred to him in a letter to Coutts as "my peculiar protégé among the smaller fry"; when he was twelve he was "*the* boy of the lot.") He, like Alfred, was named after an eminent figure—the brilliant late ecclesiastic Sydney

Smith, known equally for his trenchant wit and reformist ideas.

It was apparently a difficult and prolonged breech birth—"My dear Kate suffered terribly," Dickens at once wrote to Macready—but mother and baby recovered in good fashion. From the very beginning, Sydney was tiny, the tiniest of an almost uniformly short family, but he was energetic and intrepid. Dickens reports him at three with "A fresh wind blowing, and nearly blowing him off his legs in the garden—His hair all over his face—his hat nowhere in particular—and he lugging a seat about—equal in weight, I should think, to six legs of mutton."

A family anecdote involves the three-year-old boy being sent off by his father, as a joke, to the railroad station to meet Forster. A forceful "Yes" from Sydney and he's out through the garden gate and off down the road until he's rounded up and brought back. Dickens and the rest of the family now take up a game of letting him rush out into the street and then hauling him back, until, with his older brother Alfred (now five) in tow, he *isn't* hauled back—Dickens, in fun, has shut the garden gate and hidden with the others. In a letter to Catherine he goes on with the story: "Presently, we heard them come back and say to each other with some alarm, 'Why, the gate's shut, and they are all gone!' Ally began in a dismayed way to cry out, but the Phenomonon [*sic*], shouting 'Open the gate!' sent an enormous stone flying into the garden (among our heads) by way of alarming the establishment." This was a boy after his father's heart.

Very early he was nicknamed "The Ocean Spectre" because of what Georgina called his curious habit of pausing in his play, cupping his tiny hands under his chin, and casting a faraway look over the ocean. At such times, she reported, a film seemed to pass over his eyes, as if, Dickens laughingly suggested, he were entertaining a "clear vision of futurity." The nickname stuck: he was still the Ocean Spectre (in baby talk reduced to "Hoshen Peck") or simply the Spectre into his adulthood.

When he was eight, he was sent off to school in Boulogne to join Alfred and Frank, and very soon he had made up his mind that he wanted to go to sea. Unlike so many of his brothers, he knew from the start exactly what he meant to be, and he was unswerving in his determination. When he's eleven, his father is writing to his schoolmasters,

Will you . . . tell me whether you think the gigantic Sydney really has any sort of Call to the Sea Service? He has often talked of it at home here, and has lately written an odd characteristic letter to one of his sisters, entreating her to ask me to make the Navy his profession, as he is devoted to it "without any sham" and longs to follow it. I cannot make out in my own mind, how much of this ardour is in-bred in the boy, and how much of it is referable to the frequent appearances here, in the last holidays, of a young Midshipman, the son of an Edinburgh friend of mine, in glorious buttons and with a real steel weapon in his belt . . . he is a boy of such remarkable energy and purpose, considering his years and inches, that if I supposed him to be quite in earnest and to have made up his mind, I would give him his way, because I really believe he would then follow it out with spirit.

Having one of his sons display "such remarkable energy and purpose" obviously pleased Dickens, and he decided to allow Sydney to pursue his goal in life, writing to the head of the naval school,

> One of my boys, at present not quite twelve years of age, has chosen the Navy for his profession. As I do not doubt his being able to pass his examinations as soon as he is old enough, if he be trained in the meantime with an immediate and direct view to the pursuit on which he has set his heart, will you permit me to enquire if you can receive him into your house and take him under your care at Easter next? He is now at school in Boulogne. His name is Sydney Smith. He is a boy of very remarkable strength of character, of great intelligence, and of a most indomitable energy. I am as little prejudiced (I believe) as a father can be in forming my opinion of my sons; but I think you will be interested in him, and that he will not do injustice to your reputation.

Sydney proceeds to the naval school in Portsmouth, where he does well, and his father uses his connections with the Admiralty to procure him a nomination as a naval cadet. "My son will be thirteen years of age on the 18th of next April. As he has been well trained for his profession, his tutor at Portsmouth informs me that he will be quite competent to pass the examination, in March, and that he believes the new regulations will admit of his going up then, instead of waiting until after his thirteenth birthday and going up in June."

In September, Dickens writes to a friend, "Sydney has just passed his examination as a Naval cadet, and come home, all eyes and gold buttons." And Wilkie Collins informs his mother about Sydney's arrival from Portsmouth: "He had a glass of Champagne, and we took him to the Theatre immediately, by way of encouraging one of our naval heroes." On September 24, Dickens writes to Georgina, after having escorted his son back to Portsmouth and his training ship, "At the Waterloo Station we were saluted with 'Hallo! *Here's* Dickens!' from divers naval Cadets." And, "The moment we stepped on board, 'Hul-lo *Here's* Dickens!' was repeated on all sides; and the Admiral [Sydney] (evidently very popular) shook hands with about fifty of his messmates . . . There is no denying that he looks very small aboard a great ship, and that a boy must have a strong and decided specialty for the sea to take to such a life." To his master at the naval school, Dickens writes, "The gallant Sydney is in immense repute at Portsmouth, and is shewn to visitors, as one of the curiosities of the place. When he is in the country with me, he usually lives up a tree or on the top of a pole." It seems that at the naval college he is generally referred to as "Young Dickens who can do anything."

Dickens found Sydney perpetually amusing, making fond jokes about "the Admiral's" diminutive size. "His sextant (which is about the size and shape of a cocked hat), on being applied to his eye, entirely concealed him. Not the faintest trace of the distinguished office behind it was perceptible to the human vision."

After finishing his course on his training ship, Sydney was appointed to the *Orlando* ("the finest ship in the service I believe," boasted his father) and sailed instantly for America. He was fourteen, and of course looked far younger, given his diminutive stature—barely over five feet tall. (He could easily have lived in his sea chest, Dickens remarked.) He was a particular pet of Dickens's great friend the artist John

Leech, who in later years would take him to dinner at the Garrick after each cruise, and once interfered when he saw Sydney trying to eat with the huge silver knife that had been provided. When the waiter brought them smaller silverware, "he and the officer messed with great satisfaction, and agreed that things in general were running too large in England."

Georgina was less sanguine about Sydney than his father was: "We shall not see him again for three years, I fear. It is sad work." But though his letters were dejected at first, "he writes now in better spirits," and "is cheerful in his projects." Catherine, also, missed him badly. They had always been close. Writing to her sister Helen in 1858, after Dickens had taken the children away from her, she noted that "little Sydney was full of solicitude and anxiety about me, always asking what I should do when they were gone, and if I would not be very dull and lonely without them; he should so like to stay." When he was older and home from his voyages, he would be with her a great deal in London—and indeed he left all his money to her in his will.

Reports of his career are uniformly positive. Dickens is again boasting of him in 1862: He's "a born little sailor . . . and will make his way anywhere." A few years later he's telling Lord Russell, "I am happy to report that my sailor-boy's captain . . . departs from the mere form of certificate given to all the rest, and adds that his obedience to orders is remarkable, and that he is a highly intelligent and promising young officer." In 1867, Sydney unexpectedly turns up in London from Portsmouth, having just been made a lieutenant, "with the consequent golden garniture on his sleeve," wrote Dickens. "Which I, God forgive me, stared at without the least idea that it meant promotion." To Macready Dickens wrote,

"My boy Sydney is now a Second Lieutenant: the youngest in the service, I believe. He has the highest testimonials as an officer."

However, he goes on: "But I fear he has an inveterate habit of drawing bills, that will ruin him." The (assumed) hereditary strain of irresponsibility with money, already manifest in Walter and Alfred and Frank as well as in Dickens's father and brothers, emerged in full force, and very early, in Sydney. Within a year there were tales of his behavior in Bermuda, where he made "prodigious purchases of luxuries"—guava jelly, rahat-lakoum (Turkish delight), bananas, boot laces—to the gratification of "the coloured bumboat woman [as per Georgina] Mrs. Dinah Browne," who apparently had him to tea with her on shore, where she entertained him "with charming coon-songs in a rich . . . contralto voice."

Sydney's reckless spending continued through the sixties, earning him reproaches from his father that evoked apologies and repentance, and promises that were never kept. In 1868, Dickens warned one of Sydney's creditors, "I recognize no bills drawn upon me, or for my son Mr. Sydney Smith Dickens, R.N. I recognize no bills drawn upon me, or upon you, now that my son is of age." Yet over the next eighteen months or so he paid this creditor close to £175. It was during this period that he wrote to George Dolby, his friend and the manager of his reading tours, "I can't get my hat on; in consequence of the extent to which my hair stands on end at the costs and charges of these boys. Why was I ever a father! Why was *my* father ever a father!"

In 1869, Dickens learned that on leaving Vancouver Island, Sydney had drawn heavily on his agents, telling his father that unless his bills were paid, his professional career would be severely damaged. "You can't imagine how ashamed I am to appeal to you again . . . If any promises for future amends can be relied on you have mine most cordially, but for God's sake assist me now, it is a lesson I am not likely to forget if you do and if you do not I *can* never forget. The result of your refusal is terrible to *think* of." Again Dickens came to the rescue, but his anger and disappointment grew. Georgina, much as she cared for the boys, was always most concerned for the father. The failure of Sydney was, she felt, the hardest for him to bear, the Ocean Spectre having always been the favorite boy, and the most promising.

After all the crises, warnings, broken promises, and stronger and stronger reproofs, Dickens finally drew the line and, Georgina sadly informed Annie Fields, forbade his beloved son to appear at Gad's Hill when he should return to England.

Saddest and cruelest of all was his writing to Alfred in May 1870, "I fear Sydney is much too far gone for recovery, and I begin to wish that he were honestly dead." This to Sydney's brother! Less than three weeks later, Dickens himself was dead.

HENRY

Sir Henry Fielding Dickens, 1849–1933

HENRY FIELDING DICKENS, named after one of his father's favorite novelists, was certainly the most successful of the Dickens children, and was probably the happiest. He also had the distinction of thoroughly pleasing his loving but exacting father. From the moment he determined his professional path, he rose steadily upward; not, perhaps, to the very top, but to honors, the high respect of his colleagues, and considerable remuneration. He was blessedly fortunate in his marriage, and his numerous children proved sound and

satisfying, though one son was to die in the First World War—
the only real tragedy of Henry's life. It was as if all the good
luck the fairies had available for the Dickens family found its
way to him. Even his early nicknames—"The Jolly Postboy"
and "The Comic Countryman" (later, he would be Mr. H, or
just H)—suggest what a jolly and comical lad he was.

He was also a kind and generous man, and available to a
good time—something of a (very proper) man about town, and
something of an avid traveler. Not many men "went up in the
air," as he put it, for the first time at the age of eighty-two, glee-
fully flying over the Panama Canal with his son and grandson.

His birth had not been so gleeful. Henry, Dickens wrote
to Macready, had not

come into the world as he ought to have done (I don't
know in what we have offended Nature, but she seems to
have taken something in us amiss) and we had to call in
extra counsel and assistance. Foreseeing the possibility of
such a repetition of last time, I had made myself thoroughly acquainted in Edinburgh with the *facts* of chloro-
form—in contradistinction to the talk about it—and had
insisted on the attendance of a gentleman from Bar-
tholomew's Hospital, who administers it in the operations there, and has given it four or five thousand
times . . . The doctors were dead against it, but I stood my
ground, and (thank God) triumphantly. It spared her all
pain (she had no sensation, but of a great display of sky-
rockets) and saved the child all mutilation.

Harry, indeed, emerged "a Moon-faced monster."
By the time the boy was five, he had been swept up in the

annual amateur theatricals that dominated the Christmas–Twelfth Night weeks in the Dickens household. Dickens himself arranged a version of *Tom Thumb* in which little Harry stole the show with his rendition of a famous comic song:

Now comes the conflabbergastation of the lovier:
As Vilikins was valiking the garden around
He spied his dear Dinah laying dead upon the ground,
And a cup of cold pison it lay by her side,
With a billet-dux a-stating 'twas by pison she died.
Too ral lal, lo oral lal, too ral la.

Thackeray, there for the festivities with his two young daughters, is said to have fallen off his chair with laughter at this performance. And the next year Harry—"who created so Powerful an Impression last year"—was back again, this time in something called *Fortunio and His Seven Gifted Servants: A Fairy Extravaganza*. The theatricals were run by Dickens with his customary rigor and perfectionism, also expressed, as the boys grew older, in his rules for domestic behavior. "A system was set on foot," wrote Henry in his *Recollections*, "which went by the name of 'Pegs, Parade, and Custos.' To each boy was allotted a particular peg for his hat and coat: there was a parade from time to time, in order to check the stains of grease or dirt which had accumulated on our clothing; and to one boy was allotted the task each week of collecting the sticks, balls and croquet and cricket materials which represented the 'Custos' for the week. We shied a little at this kind of discipline on the first going off, but we soon fell into line and rather enjoyed it than otherwise."

When he was nine, Harry was sent off to the school in

Boulogne where two of his brothers were still ensconced, but as he would write, "I cannot say I look back on my days there with any degree of pleasure. I did not quite like dining off tin plates, nor was the food altogether appetising"—hardly surprising when it most often consisted of "very pale veal with very, very watery gravy and the usual stick-jaw pudding." When his youngest brother, Plorn, followed him to Boulogne and was unhappy, both boys were brought back home.

This was at the very time when the Dickens household was being torn apart by Charles's determination to be separated from Catherine. Like his brothers and sisters, Henry was always reticent on this subject, only commenting in his *Recollections*, "All I desire to say about it is this: that both in my father's lifetime, with his full knowledge and acquiescence, as well as after his death, I used regularly to visit my dear mother at her house in Gloucester Crescent, Regent's Park, and that we lived on terms of mutual affection until her death in the year 1879."

It was also then that Dickens and his brood, with Georgina in charge ("one of the dearest friends I ever had," Henry would write), took up permanent residence in Gad's Hill, and then that Harry was sent to the Wimbledon School, where several of his older brothers had gone. Wimbledon was meant primarily as a jumping-off place for a military life or for preparation for the Indian Civil Service, but Harry was not interested in either of these professions.

His memoirs remind us that for him and the other younger Dickens children Gad's Hill was a paradise of happy domestic gatherings, an endless procession of fascinating and amiable visitors and guests, sporting activities, long healthy walks, almost a menagerie of family pets, and the brilliant, usually buoyant presence of their father in charge of everything. One

diversion which took on an almost professional aspect was the
family newspaper the boys started up and ran by themselves.

It was a small undertaking at first, as all "big" things are;
indeed I may say very small. But, though the undertaking was small in itself, we had a large and most enlight-
ened staff. An editor who had nothing to edit, a writer
who wrote nothing, an office boy and a bell. The bell did
most of the work. I was the boy and the bell was contin-
ually rung for my attendance, though why I was wanted
I never quite understood. However, it all looked very imposing, and that was all we cared about.

The outcome of this gallant show was the issue, every
week, of one ordinary sheet of notepaper containing an
account in writing of the ongoing life at Gad's Hill ["H
Dickens is the present champion at billiards." August 5,
1865]. Little by little the number of sheets was increased
by means of a manifold writer; and at last, when I was
the only member of the company left, Mr. Wills, the
sub-editor of *All the Year Round*, presented me with a real
working printing press, complete with all necessary type
and other accessories. I at once proceeded to learn the art
of printing at the large printing establishment, Beaufort
House in the Strand; and it was not long before I mas-
tered the necessary processes of "composing," "typing,"
"tightening-up the chases," and so forth, necessary to
produce the printed sheet. The paper scheme now assumed a very different aspect, for, ceasing to be a mere
part of childish play-acting, it became a matter of really
hard and continuous labour. I worked it entirely by myself . . . I first of all had to collect the items of news of

what had occurred during the week, not only at Gad's Hill itself, but in the surrounding neighbourhood, write a modest little leader, set up the type, print the copies, address, stamp and post them and finish up by "distributing" and cleaning the type for use on the next edition. It really took up the whole of my week; but it was quite an interesting job and I enjoyed it.

What matters about *The Gad's Hill Gazette* is that it indicates just how hard-working and capable the young Henry was, how determined to learn the hard way and to see things through. To Dickens it must have been balm, considering how consistently disappointed he was in the other boys, how feckless they seemed to him, with Plorn, the youngest of them, perhaps lacking to the greatest extent the life-force and drive he felt were essential for a man, and of which he himself had such an extraordinary supply.

Harry had decided that he wished to go to Cambridge to study for the legal profession, but his father was cautious—he had been disappointed in his sons too many times by now. Writing to the Rev. J. M. Brackenbury at Wimbledon, Dickens—who had previously written to him about Harry, "His quickness in learning, I observed to be remarkable when he was a mere baby"—now asked him "to tell me whether you believe he really will be worth sending to Cambridge, and really has the qualities and habits essential to marked success there." The response was positive, and it was arranged for Harry to go up to Trinity Hall, a law college, in 1869.

But not before Dickens had consulted a knowledgeable friend, explaining that Henry "has been highly educated—is

III

Henry Dickens

possessed of considerable mathematical qualifications—and goes to College to work, and to achieve distinction. He perfectly understands that if he fails to set to in earnest, I shall take him away," and goes on to ask, "Will you tell me what the allowance of such a youth should be, at Cambridge—to be enough, and not by any means too much?" To Henry himself, soon after his arrival at college, Dickens writes, "You know how hard I work for what I get, and I think you know that I never had money help from any human creature after I was a child. You know that you are one of the many heavy charges on me, and that I trust to your so exercising your abilities and improving the advantages of your past expensive education, as soon to diminish *this* charge."

And, "Now observe attentively. We must have no shadow of debt. Square up everything whatsoever that it has been necessary to buy. Let not a farthing be outstanding on any account, when we begin with your allowance. Be particular in the minutest detail." The allowance was £250 a year, to cover all expenses except Harry's wines, which were ordered and sent to Cambridge: three dozen sherry, two dozen port, six bottles of brandy, and three dozen light claret.

And so, armored against further disappointment—fearing the worst, hoping for the best—Dickens sent his one supremely industrious son off to university.

From the start he was a success, beginning with his first speech at the Union, the Cambridge debating society. ("My dear Harry. I am extremely glad to hear that you have made a good start at the Union. Take any amount of pains about it, open your mouth well and roundly, speak to the last person visible, and give yourself time." Dickens himself, of course, was a brilliant public speaker.) Soon he had won a £50 scholarship. (Dickens to Forster: "I have a great success in the boy-line to announce to you.") The £50, needless to say, went to reducing Harry's allowance.

Dickens's reception of the news of this scholarship meant so much to Harry that he told the story both in his brief *Memories of My Father* and his later *Recollections*. "I met him in the train at Higham Station to tell him what had happened," goes the second of these accounts, "and I gave him the news as he alighted from the train. He said, 'Capital! Capital!' that was all. I was, I must confess, somewhat disappointed at this rather luke-warm treatment of my news; but my father could not for long maintain this apparently cold attitude. Half-way up the road to Gad's Hill he completely broke down. Turning to me with tears in his eyes he gave me a grip of the hand, which I can almost feel now and he said, 'God bless you, my boy, God bless you.'" We can allow ourselves to share in Harry's pride in having pleased his father and Dickens's pride and relief in having a satisfactory—a successful—son. As Georgina put it, "It is a famous beginning . . . and I hope augurs well for his future college career. It will be quite a new sensation for Charles to have one of his sons distinguish himself."

Harry's Cambridge years were a total pleasure to him. His academic record was excellent, and he reveled in the social and sporting life—coxing for Trinity and becoming an important figure in the cricket world. (He also organized, at Gad's Hill, a vigorous cricket club for the family and the town.) "I can look back at my Varsity life with unqualified pleasure," he would write in his old age, "and in order to show how greatly attached I was to the college, I may add that I sent three of my sons there afterward, which must, I think, be quite a record." It is all such a far cry from the fates of the five of his brothers who were dispatched by their father around the world.

After Harry's success, the relations between father and son "became closer and warmer than they had even been before, and when New Year's Eve came, the year before he died, and he clasped my hand to wish me a Happy New Year, there was a steady look in his eye which I read as meaning, 'We understand one another; I trust you to try to do your best in life.'"

Early in 1870, Dickens gave a small dinner party to celebrate Harry's coming of age. It was obvious to everyone by then that Dickens's health was eroding, but he was only fifty-eight and no one suspected that the end was so near. Harry was at college in June when he received an urgent letter from Georgina and his sisters saying that his father had suffered a massive stroke and was not expected to live. "Almost stupefied with grief," he rushed home, arriving two hours after his father died, and heard the news at the station when his train got in.

His love and admiration for his father never left him. "If I was asked, when all is said and done, what is my most abiding memory of him, I should say, beyond all question, it was of his lovable and great-hearted nature." And on the first page of his *Recollections*—published in 1934, the year after his death—he wrote, "During the latter years of my father's life my whole being was engrossed in his; and since his death I live upon my memory of him, which is a very deep and living thing."

DORA

Dora Annie Dickens, 1850–1851

W HEN ON AUGUST 16, 1850, Catherine Dickens gave
birth to her ninth child, it was her fifth confinement
in less than seven years. The baby was frail, and Catherine
equally so—her post-partum depressions and physical lassitude had grown stronger over the years. Soon she was suffering from what Dickens described as "an alarming disposition
of the blood to the head, attended by giddiness and dimness
of sight," a recurring condition Dickens considered more men-
tal than physical.

In February, when Dora was six months old, she fell so ill
with what Dickens called "something like congestion of the
brain" that she was baptized immediately, reducing her mother
to a state of nervous collapse. The following month, leaving
the baby, who seemed restored to health, to the care of her
husband and the nurse, Catherine, accompanied by Georgina, withdrew to rest, recuperate, and take the famously
pure waters at the Great Malvern spa, in Worcestershire.
(Even today, Great Malvern's bottled water is the only brand
used by the Queen.)

Within a month she received word from Dickens that Dora, unexpectedly and with no warning, had been stricken by a serious illness and might not live. Actually, Dora was already dead, but Dickens felt it important that Catherine be allowed to take in this dire news gradually.

> Now observe. You must read this letter, very slowly and carefully. If you have hurried on this far without quite understanding (apprehending some bad news), I rely on your turning back, and reading again. Little Dora, without being in the least pain, is suddenly stricken ill. She awoke out of a deep sleep, and was seen in one moment, to be very ill. Mind! I will not deceive you. I think her *very* ill. There is nothing in her appearance but perfect rest. You would suppose her quietly asleep . . . I do not— why should I say I do, to you my dear!—I do not think her recovery at all likely . . . if—*if*—when you come, I should even have to say to you "our little baby is dead," you are to do your duty to the rest, and to shew yourself worthy of the great trust you hold in them.

Forster was sent to Malvern to hand Catherine this tender letter and to bring her and Georgina home; perhaps Dickens thought it was more important to stay with the other children at so tragic a moment than to bring the news himself to his wife and try to comfort her. He had been very attentive to her during her stay in Malvern, going down to be with her more than once at a time of grave problems of his own—only a fortnight before Dora's death his lovable and maddening father had died after a terrible operation: "He bore it with astonishing fortitude, and I saw him directly afterwards—his room, a slaughter house of blood."

On April 14, Dickens had returned to London from Malvern in order to preside over a dinner for the benefit of the General Theatrical Fund. He had spent the afternoon at home, according to Mamie's account, "playing with the children and carrying little Dora about the house and garden." When he left for the London Tavern, the baby was apparently in perfectly good health ("I had left her well and gay," he wrote to Coutts), but by the time he was preparing to launch the festivities, a Dickens servant had arrived and summoned Forster out of the room with the awful news that Dora had succumbed within minutes of an attack of "convulsions." Only at the close of the proceedings did Forster, with the support of another intimate friend, Mark Lemon, break the news to Dickens, who rushed home and, with Forster and Lemon, sat all night by his little girl's body.

Catherine, on returning home to learn that Dora was indeed dead, was overwhelmed with grief, but some days later, after the funeral, Dickens could report to Edward Bulwer-Lytton that she was as well as he could hope—resigned, and able to "speak of it tranquilly." According to Mamie, however, a day or two earlier Dickens himself "suddenly gave way completely" when he was about to take some flowers upstairs "and place them on the little dead baby." Mamie also quotes her father as saying, "We laid the child in her grave today. And it is part of the goodness and mercy of God that if we could bring her back to life, now, with a wish, we would not do it." There are things about the Victorians that we will never understand.

Just as inexplicable, at least to me, is his choice of the name Dora for this child. At the time of her birth he was feverishly working on *David Copperfield*, and as he wrote to Catherine, "I still have Dora to kill—I mean the Copperfield Dora—and cannot make certain how long it will take to do." The real Dora was born, and a week later the fictional one was dead. Forster, in his biography, suggests that Dickens may have hoped to give some posthumous life to the loving, foolish child-wife he had created for his book and who was one of his favorite characters, but nothing can really explain naming one's newborn after a character you are in the process of killing off. What can Catherine have made of this? But, then, Catherine was never allowed to participate in the naming of her babies.

The bereaved parents distracted themselves somewhat by searching for a new London residence, and slowly they emerged from their grief for "our poor little pet," as Dickens called her. "I am quite happy again," he was able to write after some time had passed, "but I have undergone a great deal."

PLORN

Edward Bulwer Lytton Dickens, 1852–1902

Dickens to Wills, March 13, 1852: "I am happy to say that Mrs. Dickens is just confined with a brilliant boy of unheard-of-dimensions." But six days later he is writing to another friend declaring himself uncertain whether he had "particularly wanted" the baby, yet acknowledging that the baby might be "good for me in some point of view or other." The boy was named after his friend the famous novelist Bulwer-Lytton (the first Baron Lytton), author of a series of tremendous bestsellers including *The Last Days of Pompeii*, *Rienzi*, *Eugene Aram*, and *Paul Clifford*, the first line of which is the endlessly parodied "It was a dark and stormy night." He was, after Dickens, the most popular novelist of the period, and their friendship and professional relationship lasted until Dickens's death: Dickens serialized Bulwer-Lytton's novels in *All the Year Round*, and so respected his talent and judgment that he accepted his advice to modify the original sad ending of *Great Expectations*.

Baby Edward soon became Plorn, the name he was known by throughout his life, "Edward" used only for official pur-

Edward "Plorn" Dickens

poses. And Plorn indeed proved to be good for his father, a particular favorite, even for some while replacing Katey as his *absolute* favorite. To Coutts, when Plorn is just one: "I think that must be all a mistake about that Suffolk baby your nephew, because (it is a remarkable fact) we have in this house the only baby worth mentioning; and there cannot possibly be another baby anywhere, to come into competition with him. I happen to know this, and would like it to be generally understood." Even before he was three, Plorn was trotted onto the home stage to appear in the family's annual Twelfth Night play; the program—written, of course, by Dickens—announces the fantastically named "Mr. Plornishmaroontigoonter, who has been kept out of bed at a vast expense." (Mamie tells us he "was so small that he could hardly stand in the little top-boots that were made for him.) This outlandish moniker shrank to "The Plornishgenter" before settling down for life as Plorn.

In the early 1850s, summers were spent on the French coast, from where Dickens writes to a friend that the "beauty, size and vigour of the Baby" were "the admiration of the entire population of Boulogne without any distinction of race or country." Another letter seconds this verdict: "The Plornish Maroon is in a brilliant state, beating all former babies into what they call in America (I don't know why) sky-blue fits." Mamie, in her memoir of her father, recalls that at Boulogne, "He would often have his youngest boy, 'The Noble Plorn,' trotting at his side. These two were constant companions in those days, and after these walks my father would always have some funny anecdote to tell us." Something about Plorn just tickled Dickens. Mamie also had "the remembrance of these two, hand in hand, the boy in his white frock and blue sash, walking down the avenue, always in deep conversation," and of Dickens at a fair in Boulogne carrying "his last baby-boy on his shoulders or on his head all the way." ("Perhaps the last time we shall have a vision of the relaxed Dickens," comments Peter Ackroyd.)

When Plorn is five he's promoted to trousers, his Aunt Georgina wanting to postpone the great day until Charles could be home from a reading tour to witness the occasion, but Dickens writes, "My best love to the noble Plornish. If he is quite reconciled to the postponement of his trousers, I should like to behold his first appearance in them. But, if not, as he is such a good fellow, I think it would be a pity to disappoint and try him."

We have no comparable vignettes concerning Dickens and his other little boys, however much he may have loved them. His partiality was noted by the others: both Mamie and Harry refer to Plorn as their father's favorite, with no apparent resentment or jealousy. This child—humorous, shy, even timorous—was apparently adored by everyone.

Plorn's shyness, though, began to affect his childhood. Harry, his elder by three years, was at school in Boulogne, but as we have seen, he was brought home because Plorn needed his companionship, and Boulogne, so far from home, was clearly not right for him. The two boys were enrolled in a Rochester grammar school near Gad's Hill. Dickens to Georgina: "Plorn's admission that he likes the school very much indeed, is the great social triumph of modern times." But when the boys moved on to the Wimbledon School, it was not long before the eleven-year-old—described as "sensitive and unaggressive" by Georgina's biographer—told his father that the large school confused him and asked to be removed from it.

It was then decided to place him in a private situation with only a few other pupils. Writing to the Rev. W. C. Sawyer, in November 1863, Dickens says: "He is a shy boy of good average abilities, and an amiable disposition. But he has not been quite happy away from home, through having lived—as the youngest of my children—a little too long at home with grown people. He has never been a spoiled child however, for we are too fond of our children here to make them disagreeable. He was at Wimbledon school with his brother until within these six months, but he told me he found so large a school confusing. He had always an excellent character there, and I feel sure he is a good boy whose confidence could be easily won by the spirit in which you address your charges."

By the time Plorn was fifteen, Dickens had hardened his opinion of his best-loved boy, whose fatal "want of application" was an ongoing theme in his analysis of his son, and had concluded that—as with Walter, Sydney, Frank, and Alfred—a vigorous life overseas was the right path for him. The decision was made that he would follow Alfred to Australia. (An ambiguous letter to Georgie suggests that Catherine had protested this decision, but of course she had no legal right to interfere with it.)

To one of Plorn's preceptors Dickens wrote,

I thoroughly concur with you touching the expedience of giving Edward's education during the ensuing term, a practical direction immediately bearing on the way of life before him. I quite approve of his discontinuing Latin, and devoting the time so gained to History, Natural philosophy, and a general improvement of his acquaintance with the properties of the things that he will have to subdue to his use in a rough wild life. But . . . His want of application and continuity of purpose would be quite extraordinary to me if I had not observed the same defect in one of his brothers [probably Frank] and tried to trace it to its source. [The source, in his view, was Catherine, whom Dickens criticized privately and publicly for her lethargy and indolence.] That a certain amount of unsatisfactory and impracticable torpor is in his natural character, and is consequently his misfortune, I am sure. But he will have more pressing need to make a fight against it in Australia than if he were near home; and as he is fond of animals, and of being on horseback and of moving rapidly through the air, I hope he may take better to the Bush than to Books. His natural abilities may flare up, under such conditions.

To help prepare him for sheep-raising and farming, Plorn was dispatched to the agricultural college in Cirencester. "Tell Plorn, with my love," Dickens wrote to Georgina from America, "that I think he will find himself much interested in that college, and that it is very likely he may make some acquaintances there that will hereafter be pleasant and useful to him." To Alfred, Dickens had written that since Plorn's

mind is quite made up to try Bush life in earnest, I have arranged that he should come out to you as to arrive in Melbourne about Christmas—as you recommend . . . You will find him able to turn his hand to a good many things. He can ride, do a little carpentering, make a horse's shoe, and job handily in various ways. He has some little knowledge of chemistry also. He is well grown and strong, and has many requisites for the life, *if* he take to it steadily. By this expression, I don't mean that he is in the least likely to go wild or do wrong; I simply mean that he may not take to the life when he comes face to face with it. Of that, we can form no accurate judgment until he tries it. You will observe him, and will soon see how he tends.

It's easy to condemn Dickens for pushing the sensitive Plorn so violently out of the nest, but at least the boy was consulted and apparently was content with the arrangement: Alfred was happy in Australia, and of course it was an adventure. Perhaps, as well, Plorn was on some level relieved at the idea of living far from his father's critical gaze. Mary Lazarus, author of an invaluable book on the careers of the two Dickens sons in Australia (*A Tale of Two Brothers*), writes, "His father might have made the suggestion in the first place, but it is improbable that he would have forced his beloved child to go against his will. He was a dominating father, but not a tyrannical one"—a just verdict, it seems to me. Even so, if Boulogne was too far from the family, and a normal school too confusing for a shy boy, how could Dickens have expelled him from home and halfway around the world, however wanting in application he may have been?

The parting was deeply painful. Dickens and Harry conveyed Plorn to the railroad station from which, escorted by Harry, he would travel to Plymouth; the sailing ship *Sussex* would depart from there to Australia in the fall of 1868. More than half a century later, Harry would write in his memoirs,

I shall never forget, so long as I live, the parting which took place between my father and my brother Edward, his youngest and best loved son, when he left home for Australia in September 1868. I accompanied my brother to Plymouth to see him off in one of Green's sailing ships, and was on the platform of Paddington Station when the parting took place. I never saw a man so completely overcome, giving way, as [my father] did, to extreme sorrow, quite unconscious of his surroundings on the platform.

Later that day, Dickens reported to Mamie,

I can honestly report that he went away, poor dear fellow, as well as could be expected. He was pale and had been crying, and (Harry said) had broken down in the railway carriage after leaving Higham station; but only for a short time. Just before the train started he cried a good deal but not painfully . . . these are hard, hard things but they might have to be done without means or influence, and then they would be far harder. God bless him!

To Fechter he wrote, "Poor Plorn has gone to Australia. He seemed to me to become once more my youngest and favourite little child as the day drew near, and I did not think I could have been so shaken."

Catherine had already written her son a long letter so that when he arrived in Melbourne he would find it waiting for him: "I miss you most sadly, my own darling Plorn." Katey wrote as well, hoping he would remember them and "above all dear Papa, and make his name more honoured than it is already." It would seem that all of them apart from Catherine, and including Dickens himself, were more concerned with his feelings than with Plorn's.

As he had done with his other sons as they left home, Dickens wrote a long letter for Plorn to take with him.

My dearest Plorn, I write this note today because your going away is much upon my mind, and because I want you to have a few parting words from me, to think of now and then at quiet times. I need not tell you that I love you dearly, and am very, very, sorry in my heart to part with you. But this life is half made up of partings, and these pains must be borne. It is my comfort and my sincere conviction that you are going to try the life for which you are best fitted. I think its freedom and wildness more suited to you than any experiment in a study or office would have been; and without training, you could have followed no other suitable occupation.

What you have always wanted until now has been a set, steady, constant purpose. I therefore exhort you to persevere in a thorough determination; to do whatever you have to do as well as you can do it. I was not so old as you are now, when I first had to win my food, and to do it out of this determination and I have never slackened in it since.

Never take a mean advantage of anyone in any transaction, and never be hard upon people who are in your power. Try to do to others, as you would them do to you, and do not be discouraged if they fail sometimes. It is much better for you that they should fail in obeying the greatest rule laid down by Our Saviour than that you should.

After considerable further exhortation about Christianity and the need never to "abandon the wholesome practice of saying your own private prayers, night and morning. I have never abandoned it myself, and I know the comfort of it," he ends, "I hope you will always be able to say in after life, that you had a kind father. You cannot show your affection for him so well, or make him so happy, as by doing your duty." In other words, Plorn is to lead a good life for his father's sake, not his own. But then Dickens was always center stage, no matter what stage he was on or who was on it with him.

The *Sussex* sailed on October 2, 1868. Several weeks later, Dickens wrote to Annie Fields:

> The latest Gad's Hill news is that my youngest boy is on his way to Australia—with an immense dog calculated to be an unspeakable comfort to the sheep, I should think! It was a sad parting, for he had been the baby all his life, and was the pet at home. He went away bravely, but we all broke down at last, I am afraid. He was completely fitted out, and had a gorgeous stern-cabin to himself, with a small armoury of rifles, revolvers, bush saddles and holsters, woodman's knives, carpenter's tools, blacksmith's tools, powder, shot, and bullets. He could make bread, brew beer, cook, hammer out a horse-shoe, and shoe a horse.

Dickens had certainly spent years worrying about Plorn and his future, and had prepared him in every possible way for this new life. And no doubt he believed that in sending his son away, he was performing a real self-sacrifice. But Plorn, he insisted, had to find his own manly way to his future, and learn to overcome those deficiencies in energy and attitude that his father deplored. It clearly never occurred to him that his disappointment—relentlessly expressed both in private and in public—over his son's temperament and performance might have made things worse. Nor was Plorn strong enough to fight back: He meekly accepted his all-powerful father's judgment of him.

Plorn arrived in Melbourne not only with his large dog but with a gift to George Rusden from his father: a complete set of his novels with a letter attached that said, "My Dear Sir, This will be presented to you by my son Edward, to whose care I have consigned the best-printed edition of my books. Let me beg of you to give them a place on your shelves, as an assurance of my friendly and grateful regard. My Dear Sir Faithfully yours always Charles Dickens."

And indeed Rusden, together with Alfred, was there to welcome the boy to Australia, first having him stay in his own home, then finding him a position as a supervisor on a sheep station far to the north and advising him never to let the men employed there grow too familiar with him: He expected Plorn always to "act as an English gentleman." Ten days after leaving for Eli Elwah, a station on the Murrumbidgee River, Plorn was back in Melbourne, with the explanation that the resident partner "was not in his opinion a gentleman," and that his opinion had become public. Not unnaturally, Rusden was troubled and disappointed at this failure of common sense, and wrote to Dickens a long account, both direct and sympathetic, of what had taken place.

So far as I can judge, your son Edward's predilections and temperament and habits are ill adapted for success in the country . . . the early rising, the attention to practical details, the strenuousness of management which imparts itself to those who are managed, the absence of repose, which characterize good managers in the country life here, are not it seems to me to be reasonably expected from your son, although he may have talent of a higher order than that which it seems to me is required in bush pursuits . . . Your son Alfred seems to possess the attributes required here; and he has displayed resolution enough to apply himself . . . I do not assert positively that [Plorn] will not show himself resolute enough and apt enough to succeed in the bush. I shall be only too glad if he does succeed for I like him very much but being intelligent and agreeable is no passport to succeed in a rough life.

Rusden found another situation for Plorn, and the young man muddled along for a year or more without settling in. The frequent letters between Rusden and Dickens followed his progress (or lack of it) with concern, exacerbated for Dickens because throughout this period his health was rapidly worsening. His final letter to Rusden was written only twenty days before his death: Plorn, he wrote, "has always been the most difficult of boys to deal with, away from home. There is not the least harm in him, and he is far more reflecting and alive *au fond* than any of his brothers. But he seems to have been born without a groove. It cannot be helped. If he cannot, or will not find one, I must try again and die trying."

Before this letter could reach Melbourne, Dickens had indeed died. Alfred wrote to Rusden that his death would "be an awful blow to poor Plorn. I have written to him and endeavored to the best of my ability to cheer him up, but I am afraid it will be a long time before he gets over the shock." We have no record of how Plorn, now eighteen, reacted to the blow.

PART TWO

1870–1933

After Dickens's death

AFTER DICKENS'S DEATH

WHEN DICKENS DIED at the age of fifty-eight, in June 1870, only four of his children were in England. Dora and Walter had died; Sydney was away at sea; Frank was in India; Alfred and Plorn were in Australia. The night he suffered his fatal stroke, as we have seen, he was alone at Gad's Hill with Georgina, who immediately summoned Mamie and Katey from London, followed the next morning by Charley. These three—the oldest of the children—waited together for his final moments, soon joined by Henry and by Ellen Ternan. When the body was brought to London and transported to Westminster Abbey for burial—without any ceremony, as Dickens had insisted—the first of the three carriages that followed the hearse from the train station held the four children; in the second were Georgina, Bessie (Charley's wife), and Laetitia, Dickens's sister. The news of his death reached the other children irregularly in those days before instant communication.

From their earliest childhoods, he had dominated their lives, both practically and emotionally; even when they were at the other ends of the earth, his approval and disapproval weighed heavily on them. The most immediately affected were, of course, those on hand, since it was up to them—and Georgina, the co-executor (with John Forster) of his will and a leading beneficiary of it—to oversee carrying out its erratic and semi-scandalous provisions, including a bequest to Ellen, provocatively set forth first and therefore highly public, and a deliberately cold and grudging reference to Catherine. The children were left equal shares of the residual funds after all obligations were discharged and all property—copyrights, real estate, etc.—turned into ready money. (By the roughest estimate, each share amounted to something like $500,000 in today's money.) Alas for the heirs, particularly Charley's eight needy offspring, copyright law was not then what it is today, or the Dickens family would have been benefiting (hugely) from his writings until well into the twentieth century.

Catherine would live on for nine more years, on easier terms with her children—making a home for Sydney when he was in England on leave, staying often and happily with Charley and his family at Gad's Hill, enjoying Henry's constant attentions to her, closer to Katey and Mamie. She had never stopped loving Dickens, and although she was devastated by his death, she emerged from her grief into a happier situation than what she would refer to as her "12 years of widowhood." And when he died she had the immediate satisfaction of a telegram of condolence from the Queen. She was still—after all, and despite all—"Mrs. Charles Dickens."

CHARLEY

In DICKENS'S WILL, Charley had been left the same share in the residual estate as the other children, as well as his father's "library of printed books, and my engravings and prints; and I also give to my son Charles the silver salver presented to me at Birmingham, and the silver cup presented to me at Edinburgh, and my shirt studs, shirt pins, and sleeve buttons." The crucial legacy, however, was that set forth in the last-minute codicil (signed on June 2, 1870, a week before Dickens died) that gave Charley his father's 90 percent share of the ownership of, and the entire responsibility for, *All the Year Round*. Clearly, Dickens had decided that his son had finally proved himself, which may well have been as great a satisfaction to Charley as the gift itself. This sudden turnabout in his prospects not only guaranteed an immediate income for Charley's ever-growing family but gave him a serious and challenging occupation, and the opportunity to win for himself a meaningful position in the literary-publishing world of the day.

Almost immediately, however, the atmosphere within the Dickens clan darkened. The dominant figure, both legally and emotionally, was Aunt Georgina, the woman who, to a

Charley Dickens

large degree, had raised the children and whom Dickens had trusted to oversee his estate and to whom he had referred in his will as "the best and truest friend man ever had." Not only did he leave her a great deal of money and his private papers, but later in the will he returned to her: "I solemnly enjoin my dear children always to remember how much they owe to the said Georgina Hogarth, and never to be wanting in a grateful and affectionate attachment to her, for they know well that she has been, through all the stages of their growth and progress, their ever useful self-denying and devoted friend."

They did remember; indeed, Kate and Mamie lived on with her—Mamie for many years, Kate after her husband,

Charlie, died—as did Henry until he married. In later days Georgina would frequently live with Henry, and to the extent that there was still a "family," she remained at the center of it as the one who communicated with everyone, passing along family news, reporting on them all to the outside world and to one another. And, like her brother-in-law, granting and withholding approval. With Charley, however, her relationship was somewhat different. Not only was he a mere ten years younger than she, but when Dickens died Charley was a grown man of thirty-three, married and already the father of a large family, who had been out in the world for a dozen or more years. (He was, for instance, the only one who called her "Gina" rather than "Auntie.") Also, he now owned *All the Year Round* and was in no way dependent on her.

The house at Gad's Hill had to be sold, and the decision was made to auction it. Georgina, together with Dickens's friend and solicitor, Frederic Ouvry, and her co-executor, John Forster, arranged for the sale, with the auctioneer instructed to accept no bid lower than £8,000, at which price the estate would buy the house for itself. What happened was either a mix-up or a calculated plot of Charley's. Forster wrote his version to Thomas Carlyle:

> Not communicating with me in any way beforehand, not knowing there was a reserved price, most unwisely and unbecomingly Charles Dickens [Charley] (representing his father alas! in no particular but his name) showed himself prominently in the crowded sale-room—very probably deterred many from bidding—and, from the slow and comparatively small offers at first made, believing (this is

his own account apologetically made to us after) that the property was about to be sacrificed, was induced to take up bidding himself—bid on, quite unconscious that he was bidding only against the auctioneer representing *us*,—and had the whole knocked down to him at the next bidding above our reserved price.

Arthur Adrian sets forth Georgina's reaction to what had happened.

How could he afford to live at Gad's Hill? Where would he raise the money to pay the estate? If, by October, he could not raise the £8,647 he had offered for the property, it would revert to the heirs, but, of course, depreciated in value. If he resold it at a loss, he would have to make up to the estate the difference between his bid and the purchase price. Should he sell it at a gain—here Georgina begins to suspect his motives. "Unless he intends that his Brothers and Sisters should share in the profit, I shall always consider it a dishonest transaction," she maintained to Frederic Ouvry, who was acting for the executors. What right, she asked, had Charley to step in, no matter how low the bids were going? "Nothing will shake my belief that Charley has taken an unfair advantage of his Brothers and Sisters in interfering with the sale of Gad's Hill *at all*," she fumed a few days later; "It would have been far better for us to leave the property *unsold* for the present—and have bought it in, for the Estate.

In the event, Charley was unable to sell or rent Gad's Hill, and for some time it stood empty. In his frantic attempts to deal with his financial difficulties, he then committed an act that to Georgina was even more deplorable than what he had done at the auction. In 1865, Dickens's friend Charles Fechter had made him a present of the prefabricated little Swiss chalet that was erected across from the main house at Gad's

Hill—the place where Katey had seen her father and embraced him for the last time. Charley, without notifying the family, sold it to be displayed at the Crystal Palace exhibition, to which it was immediately moved. Georgina to Annie Fields: "I cannot imagine *how* Charley could do such an indecent action. Also, I maintain that he had no right, to do it—without consulting the family. *Legally*, of course it was his own as he bought the property—but *morally*, he had no business to compromise *us all* . . . because when this dear sacred little place where his Father spent his last living day comes to be puffed and hawked about, ALL his family will be held responsible—and will be disgraced by it." (When Georgina's italics proliferate, you know she's up in arms.)

She and her nieces were determined to buy back the chalet if they could possibly afford it. Otherwise, they would take "steps to disavow . . . all knowledge of, and participation in, this shameful transaction." And she appealed to Fields that if she hears any mention of this "disgraceful affair," she is to "say that you *know* that to Charley Dickens *alone* belongs the discredit." She sent Ouvry to negotiate with her nephew. She refused to see him herself. She changed her own will to remove him as one of her executors. She even reduced her legacies to his daughters. "I foresee no end of family misery arising from that wretched business, all for the fault of one, and the most favoured and considered one, in the will at all events, of the children! It seems very hard and cruel, and gives me such an opinion of Charley as I am sorry to be obliged to entertain of any of his Father's children."

Fortunately for all, the Crystal Palace Company backed out of the arrangement, Charley agreed to accept £250 for the chalet, and after its repurchase, it was given to their neighbor Lord Darnley to be set up in his private garden at Cobham, where it would "be held sacred, and not exposed to being scribbled over, according to the custom of the British Public." Georgina had asked the other boys to subscribe to the repurchase, and "the Australian boys"—Alfred and Plorn—"both say *just what they ought to say* about it." Henry, of course, was of the same mind. But Frank and Sydney "have no more *feeling* in the matter than Charley has." At once she dropped the recalcitrant boys from her will. (Sydney was soon to infuriate her again, refusing to join all the others in coming to the aid of their elderly Aunt Laetitia, Dickens's much-loved sister, who was in serious financial difficulties.)

Charley earned a final black mark when he failed to discharge his responsibility to an old man, John Poole, to whom Dickens had felt an obligation to provide a respectable burial, leaving £25 for that purpose. After Poole's death, when all expenses had been paid out, there remained £10 that Georgina felt should be spent on a small headstone, but she then made a horrifying discovery: "I cannot tell you how shocked I was—as Mr. Forster was, also, to find that Charley had put old Mr. Poole into a *common* grave!" she wrote to Ouvry. "Who would have supposed he would have executed, even so small a trust, in such an indecent manner!"

How to explain this sequence of distressing acts on the part of the warm-hearted and affectionate Charley? The obvious answer is the tremendous financial pressure he was under. "To raise the purchase price of Gad's Hill," Arthur Adrian explains, "he had mortgaged the place for £5,000 and added another £3,000 from his share of the estate. Burdened with the support of a large family, forced to maintain a costly house, and faced with the diminishing income from a journal that had once flourished because of his father's prestige, he stood on perilous ground." He had already given up his home in London and moved into Gad's Hill, to gain some economic benefit from his rash purchase of it. Georgina was not persuaded. "Of course, that is his own business and no one else's," she admitted. "I surely hope the experiment will be successful."

Although *All the Year Round* was never restored to its previous great success with the public, Charley kept it going respectably for many years—resigning as its editor only in 1888 and shutting it down five years later. By all accounts, he was a considerate editor, scrupulously honest and efficient. But times had changed, tastes had changed, and the strain on him of running a publication in financial difficulties was deleterious to his always worrying health. He was by now, however, a popular and respected figure in London's literary world, especially known for his ongoing passion for the theater. And he knew everyone.

During the late seventies he wrote a series of well-researched and charmingly idiosyncratic guidebooks, the first of which—*Dickens's Dictionary of London* (1879)—was particularly successful and was followed by comparable guides to Paris, Cambridge, Oxford, and, most successfully, the Thames, all published by Charles Dickens and Evans, the firm he had established with his father-in-law.

The London dictionary is a fascination, first of all for its comprehensive if somewhat peculiar range of interests and data. The word "dictionary" is a misnomer; it's a practical guidebook, walking the reader through all the obvious subjects—museums, hospitals, parks; areas of London and its suburbs; the postal system, the police, train schedules, shopping, theaters, restaurants—but also through less practical subjects that happened to strike Charley's fancy. The writing is clear, stylish. And at times his personal reactions and biases slip into the supposedly disinterested information.

For instance, he has this to say of the Albert Hall (only eight years old at the time of writing): "The interior, which is amphitheatrical in construction—like, for example, the Coliseum at Rome—is grotesquely inappropriate to any purpose for which it is ever likely to be required. For gladiatorial exhibitions of any kind, the central area, measuring 102 ft. by 63 ft., would, of course, though rather small, be capitally adapted. A bull-fight, even, on a very small scale, might be managed here . . ." In the same spirit, he finds the equestrian statue of the Duke of Wellington "in long cloak and cocked hat, probably the most stupendous jest ever perpetrated in the way of a public monument."

There are bits of information undoubtedly more curious to us today than they seemed back then. About the postal service: "Within the limits of the Eastern Central District there are daily twelve, and within the town limits of the other districts eleven deliveries." Again: "A curiosity in the way of music-halls may be found by the explorer at the 'Bell,' in St. George street, Ratcliff-highway, where, contrary to precedent, the negro element preponderates among the audience instead of on the stage." Among the official nuisances (he refers to them as "*désagrémens*") that "will be summarily suppressed on appeal to the nearest police-constable" are carpet-beating, "dogs loose or mad," persons driving without reins, and mat-shaking after 8:00 a.m. We are instructed that if a beggar who is tormenting you is Italian, "lift your forefinger, knuckle upward, to the level of your wrist, as it hangs by your side, and wag it twice or thrice from side to side. Your Italian, who will take no other negative, accepts that instantly." We're given sensible tips on how and where to hire servants: "A serious mistake, and one too often made, is to lay down the hard-and-fast rule 'no followers allowed.' Servants always have had and always will have followers, whether their masters and mistresses like it or no. It is much wiser to recognise this fact, and to authorize the visits of the 'follower' at proper times and seasons, first taking pains to ascertain that his antecedents are good."

The most extraordinary entry is simply labeled "Jews." It explains the improvement in the condition of Jews since the various Jewish Emancipation bills of the mid-century—especially their new privilege, granted in 1871, to attend universities. "A large number of Jewish youths pass through the City of London School, whence they have carried off many of the most important prizes, scholarships, etc." The Jews have moved out in large numbers from the near-ghettoes of the East End and "taken up their quarters in Bloomsbury and Maida-vale." We learn about their work in the clothing trades, about their tastes in food. ("They love herrings steeped in brine, German sausage, the dried flesh of beef and mutton, smoked salmon, and, indeed, fish of all sorts, stewed with lemons and eggs, or fried in oil.") We learn how the Jews "slaughter their beasts . . . the butchers being an inferior sort of rabbi, who affix the seal of the synagogue to every portion of the carcase." Jews do enjoy liqueurs, but "Drunkenness . . . is an offence all but unknown." What's more, "The Jews of London are among the best fathers, sons, and husbands in the metropolis. They are a most affectionate, home-staying, sober people," charitable and devout, though "much less orthodox than formerly." And, finally, "They have no need of funeral reform, their religion enjoining the greatest simplicity in burying the dead; the use of feathers and bands is never permitted, and the coffin is always of plain unpainted and undraped wood. Thus, the Jews of London, even when ostentatious in life, practice humility in death."

What can lie behind this wide and sympathetic sociological survey of London's Jews, with whom Charley Dickens presumably had no particular connections and which is tucked away in his book among more practical data such as the address of the Guatemalan ministry and the location of a "slightly superior—or it might be more correct to say a shade less nauseating—" Opium Smoking Den? No matter. Whatever plan (if any) lay behind the erratic and often mystifying table of contents, the book was a real success, constantly reprinted, its last facsimile edition appearing as recently as 2006.

Another successful and attractive literary undertaking occupied Charley toward the end of the seventies. He was asked by the family of the late Charles James Mathews to edit and ready for publication Mathews's memoirs, letters, and speeches, a task that he accomplished swiftly, in time to be published the year after his subject's death. Mathews was not only a greatly admired comic actor but was the son of the actor (also Charles Mathews) who had been Charles Dickens's inspiration, even role model, when Dickens was a very young man addicted to the theater and thinking of becoming an actor himself—he only missed an audition for a prominent theater because of a severe cold. We know that he attended every Mathews performance possible and, more important, to some extent based the material and the tone of many of his Boz sketches on the monologues with which Mathews charmed audiences until his death in 1835, at which time his even more successful son began his forty-year career. The Mathewses, father and son, were bywords in Charley Dickens's world, and it must have been highly gratifying to him to be chosen to carry out this happy task.

The two-volume *Life of Charles James Mathews, Chiefly Autobiographical, with Selections from His Correspondence and Speeches* was published in mid-1879, going through a number of printings both in England and America, where Mathews had an ardent following. *The New York Times* of July 6, 1879, ran a 7,000-word article hailing it as the memoirs of "The most famous of English comedians in this century . . . known and admired by a wider circle than any actor of any age," and praising Charley both for his tact and modesty in allowing Mathews to speak for himself and then for bringing the story forward from the point when Mathews had stopped writing.

The book itself is completely appealing. Mathews was a charming and uninhibited writer, and his early life was filled with amusing activity, both in England and during his extensive travels in Italy, where as a young architect, his first choice of profession, he was a protégé of Lord and Lady Blessington, the fashionable, notorious mistress of the Count d'Orsay. What makes the book so particularly sympathetic is the loving, harmonious, and trusting relationship between young Charles and his parents as revealed in their voluminous correspondence. One letter from his mother to the twenty-one-year-old Charles in 1824 can stand for the entire extensive exchange:

> Neither your father nor myself wish to restrict you, my dearest Charles, in anything that can afford you present gratification or future pleasure, and you will set your bounds, which you must not altogether measure by our will to make you happy, but by your own usual discre-

tion, which we know from experience how to rely upon. Therefore, my dearest boy, make yourself quite easy and get what your prudent wishes prompt. You must be assaulted with numerous temptations to spend money, and we do not expect that you should pass everyone by, neither should we wish you to do so.

One can only speculate as to how this series of letters between such trusting and easy-going parents and their son can have affected Charley, whose own experience with a strict and disapproving father and a passive and rejected mother was so radically opposite. (At this time, Dickens had been dead only eight years and Catherine was still alive.) I like to think that, given Charley's love and veneration for his father, he felt only rapport for the protagonist of a situation that, on the surface at least, was so violently at odds with his own. Certainly, his work on the book reveals nothing but sensitivity and affinity with his subject.

Meanwhile, *All the Year Round* was staying afloat, but with considerable strain and decreasing profitability. Even now, Charley was not an effective businessman. His near-contemporary Percy Fitzgerald, who wrote for both father and son, found Charley "a perplexing fellow . . . business-like, also regular in payments, but I fancy with small control over his own expenses. For a long series of years, even to his death, he continued to baffle and surmount all difficulties."

He had given up living at Gad's Hill—it was too expensive to maintain, and the commute to his offices in London was too wearing. In 1888 he was offered a position as a reader (comparable to a senior editor today) for Macmillan's, the publisher—a job of considerable influence and one highly congenial to him. Not only was he relieved of the financial burdens and anxieties of *All the Year Round* but he was guaranteed a generous salary—more important than ever, since he had numerous grown unmarried daughters to provide for. Needless to say, these young ladies had not been educated to support themselves.

The Macmillan years were probably the most satisfying professional period of Charley's life. The firm also invited him to provide prefaces to a new edition of his father's work, an idea which, his oldest daughter was to comment, "appealed to him as no other could have done." This edition was a big and continuing success. "It would please him," his daughter went on to say, "that he should survive as writer only in connection with his father." The connection took other forms as well. Not only did he write his lively and instructive "Personal Reminiscences of My Father," of which he gave public readings in England (and which remained generally unknown until they appeared in the *Windsor Magazine* Christmas supplement issue of 1934), but he toured America with these readings, resulting in considerable profit. He also gave readings from his father's novels. By this time he and Georgina had long forgotten their differences, but at this impertinence she was not amused. "I don't profess to like the idea of Charley's reading his Father's books—and I *cannot* believe it is anything remarkable in the way of reading. Still, he has a right to do it, if he chooses—and if people are content to put money in his pocket! I can only be *very* glad. For with all those *girls*, he certainly wants as much money as he can get." Yet in the same letter to Annie Fields, she acknowledges that Charley is indeed a "good fellow."

By 1893 his health was seriously impaired, but he lingered

on until July 20, 1896, when he died at the age of fifty-nine, having lived a year longer than his father. All in all, he seems to have appreciated his life, always remembering his childhood happily, and enjoying the work he undertook once his father acknowledged that a literary life was what he was best cut out for. In her loving introduction to the published "Reminiscences," his daughter Mary Angela tells us among other things that "He was a lover of cricket and our field [at Gad's Hill] was always at the service of the village club"; that "It was as a stage-manager . . . that he reflected his father most closely . . . He absolutely revelled in the work"; that "He was essentially a good club man" with "no taste whatever for Society life. He simply found it dull." Unsurprisingly, she makes no reference to the improvidence Percy Fitzgerald commented on, nor to the dire financial situation she and her unmarried sisters found themselves in after their father's death.

And she concludes:

I have never thought it a small thing to be the granddaughter of a man whose name is known wherever the English language is spoken. I should not be my father's daughter if I were not proud of my name. But if, even to-day, my grandfather is to me someone apart from the ordinary run of men, it is because I see him still through my father's eyes. Ingrained in my father's character was an instinct for silence about which there was a great dignity. He spoke least of what he felt most. His immense pride in his father was a pride of which the very essence was reserve. My grandfather will live for me always as he was first made known to me, so many years ago, in all unconsciousness, in the devoted love and admiration of his eldest son.

Mary Angela was the only one of Dickens's grandchildren who actually remembered him—she was five when he died, and she was a favorite of his (nicknamed "Mekitty"), whose strongest memory of him was of his sitting by her bed and holding her hand, assuring her that he would make her well. She also remembered her distress when, taken to Dickens's final public reading—it was of *A Christmas Carol*—there came "the dreadful moment when he *cried*."

Mekitty would have a moderate success as a novelist and journalist, and for a short time she tried acting, but once her mother, Bessie, was gone, along with her modest pension, she and the other girls could barely scrimp by; only her sister Ethel, who opened a typing agency, had even a small measure of financial stability. By 1910 the situation was so grim that the girls made a public appeal for financial help. It was Ethel who wrote the letter begging for assistance, sending it to Lord Alverstone, Lord Chief Justice of England, and reprinting it in *The Daily Telegraph*.

My father died 15 years ago . . . my mother was subsequently granted a governmental pension of £100 a year, which on her death—three years ago—was continued to my four sisters . . . £25 a year each. Of these four sisters two (who are not at all strong or fit for work) are just barely making a living—one as a kindergarten teacher, and the other keeping a home for Indian children. The third is at present out of a post altogether, and while trying to find fresh work has nothing at all but her £15 pension, and the fourth is one of the secretaries at the National Health Society.

I myself, who am supposed to have been fairly successful—I have a copying office—have been working excessively hard for over 20 years. I have had one or two bad attacks of overwork illness, and the doctor now tells me that I have overworked for so long that six months' complete rest is imperative . . . Poverty through absolutely no fault of one's own, cannot possibly be regarded as a disgrace, and I am perfectly sure that my grandfather himself would not, were he now alive, be ashamed of us, and of any acknowledgement of our pecuniary position.

This petition had some success with the general public, but it caused extreme humiliation to the girls' Aunt Katey and Uncle Henry. According to Lucinda Hawksley (herself, as we remember, descended from Henry), "the girls' begging letter caused a family rift that lasted—between the families of Charley's and Henry's descendants—for many years."

The distressing condition in which his daughters found themselves would have been unspeakably painful for Charley—he was first and foremost a family man—but as was clear from the start, he was at his weakest dealing with money. Yet he had kept his large family afloat, and if more of his daughters had married, presumably the fate of all of them would have been easier. Or if his one son had turned out differently. In the various family memoirs and letters that appeared over the decades, no one ever mentions Charles Walter Dickens, who was born in 1865 and as a child first visited and then lived at Gad's Hill, and who should have been the natural protector of his sisters. In Claire Tomalin's recent biography of Dickens, she tells us that Charles Walter "had been disowned by the family, allegedly for marrying a bar maid called Ella Dare, and was never mentioned again, although he died in 1923." When his grandmother Catherine died, in 1879, she had left him in her will "the bronze ink-stand . . . brought me from Rome by his Uncle Sydney" and "the Ivory Elephant with Houdah sent me by his Uncle Walter"—nicely judged mementos for a fourteen-year-old boy. We can be relieved that Catherine, who had surely suffered enough, died before having to face this family disgrace.

Financial improvidence is not the greatest of failings, and on the whole, Charley's life, despite Dickens's forebodings, can be seen as a satisfying one, even a successful one. He was always a favorite with his father. His marriage was extraordinarily happy. He eventually found gratifying and rewarding occupation, and was honest, hard-working, and well-liked. His interests were diverse and wholesome. And he had a loving nature. He just wasn't his father. But then no one else was either.

MAMIE

YEARS AFTER IT HAPPENED, Mamie wrote of Dickens's death, "All through the night we watched him—my sister on one side of the couch, my aunt on the other and I keeping hot bricks to the feet that nothing could warm, hoping and praying that he might open his eyes and look at us, and know us once again. But he never moved, never opened his eyes, never showed a sign of consciousness through all the long night." The next evening, June 9, he quietly died. "I made it my business," Mamie went on, "to guard the beloved body as long as it was left us."

When Mamie's little memoir, *My Father as I Recall Him*, was published soon after her death in 1896, it made Kate wild with fury—she went through her copy of the book more than once, violently inking out passages that offended her and correcting others. When, for instance, Mamie claimed that special treatment was always given her when she was ill, Kate inserted the word "Once."

She was especially inflamed by Mamie's account of the death scene, most of all by the line about guarding the body. Guard it against whom? Georgina? Charley? Harry? Kate herself? She also noted that the boys were completely omitted from the death scene, and that their mother was allowed only one glancing reference in the entire book. And although it was here that Mamie spoke of Kate's being the "favourite" daughter, she also goes on to further her own claims: "I say this ungrudgingly, for during those last two years my father and I seemed to become more closely united, and I know how deep was the affectionate intimacy at the time of his death." Kate eliminated this entire passage in her copy of Mamie's book.

How was Mamie going to live now? She somewhat shamefacedly attempted to repair the breach with her mother, but they could not live together. Fortunately, there was sufficient money. Once the house had been auctioned off (to Charley), and the will probated, Mamie had enough to live on independently, her income soon to be augmented by Chorley's £200 annuity. In his will, Dickens had left her a share equal to that of her siblings, but as his only unmarried daughter she also received an outright legacy of £1,000 and an annuity of £300 "during her life, if she shall so long continue unmarried." On her marriage, the annuity would cease.

With Georgina she shared the sad and arduous job of closing down Gad's Hill and disposing of her father's personal possessions, and making the house ready for the upcoming sale. She was thirty-two years old, with no likelihood of marriage, no profession to pursue, no consuming interest. It made sense that at least for the immediate future she and Georgina should live together, and Georgina—"the best and truest friend man ever had," as Dickens had described her in his will—had been left a large legacy by her brother-in-law

Georgina Hogarth and Mamie Dickens

and so could enter into an appropriate financial agreement with her niece.

Within months, the two women, only eleven years apart in age, had settled into a pleasant house in Gloucester Terrace, not far from where Catherine lived. The three women maintained a formal, polite relationship, with occasional dinners and visits, but there was to be no intimacy. (Peculiarly, the daughter and her aunt remained on far warmer terms with Ellen Ternan, the mistress for whom Dickens had cast Catherine aside.) When Harry came down from Cambridge to begin his career in the law, he moved in with his sister and aunt, responsibly paying them his share of the household expenses. Even so, as Mamie spent more and more time away from London, Georgina increasingly fretted about their finances—if Mamie wasn't going to live at Gloucester Terrace, she should just move out so that Georgina could also move and live more economically. The shared household became a greater and greater financial strain as costs mounted but income did not. Georgina tells Annie Fields that they're living too expensively, "But I have not liked to thwart Mamie in this—as to worldly matters. The change to her, poor girl, is more trying than to any one, and she had expensive tastes, especially as to house and furniture, which I have not had the heart to refuse to join her in indulging." The financial situation grew more pressing when eventually Harry married and set up his own household.

Meanwhile, how was Mamie to spend her days? One idea was that she should revisit her musical studies, and a piano was acquired "as a resource and distraction," as Georgina put it, but nothing came of this. They attended musical and theatrical performances, teas and dinners, spent time with Kate and her husband when they were in London. There were endless letters to write.

Alas, a few years after her father's death Mamie sustained another blow—the death of her beloved Pomeranian, Bouncer, to whom she had been almost neurotically attached for many years, and who was well past fourteen when she died.

The inscription on the stone that marked Bouncer's grave read,

This is the Grave of
Mrs. Bouncer
The Best, the most loving, the most faithful
of little dogs.
Her happy life was passed with the exception of the last
four years of it at her home
Gad's Hill Place . . .

Mamie Dickens with Mrs. Bouncer

Among those who attempted to console Mamie was her one-time suitor Percy Fitzgerald. He had long since married, but their friendship, despite ups and downs, still mattered to them both. "I won back her favour," Fitzgerald said, "by writing and printing an ode to her little dog Bouncer." There were twelve stanzas in all, beginning "Furry, lazy, warm and bright, / Peering from her fringe of white, / She blinks and sleeps both day and night, / A happy Spitz!" and ending "Alas, so furry, warm, and white, / From this cold world she took her flight, / No more on rug by fireside bright, / Dear Bouncer sits."

It's hard not to identify with Georgina, who wrote to Annie Fields, "I did *fully* sympathize at first, and perfectly understood how much more than the usual loss of a dog the death of little Bouncer was to Mamie, but I cannot go beyond a *certain amount* of sympathy for grief over the death of an animal, and I have expressed all I have to express on the subject." She understood, nonetheless, that "It was quite extraordinary how [Bouncer's death] stirred up and reawakened *the* grief and sense of loss which is always present."

One gets, from what scant evidence exists, a sense of a rootless, purposeless life, punctuated by health problems including a frightening operation for glaucoma, which she refused to allow Kate and Georgina to see her through. She had turned in the direction of Christian social work, living for a while in Hampshire with her old friends the Humphreys, who had become strong supporters of Muscular Christianity, a movement that propagated vigorous Christian activism—that is, hands-on charity. Later, she joined her life to a shadowy couple, a clergyman and his wife named Hargreaves, who carried on philanthropic enterprises from

St. Thomas's Mission Church in Manchester. Georgina and Kate suspected the Hargreaveses of being after Mamie's money.

There were also unsubstantiated whispers of irregular sexual activities between Mamie and either (or both?) of the Hargreaveses. There was certainly far too much alcohol. Her looks were gone. In other words, Mamie's life was disintegrating. She came to London less and less frequently until eventually she agreed to dismantle her home with Georgina, which meant that there was even less contact with her aunt and sister, who worried about her ceaselessly. Georgina now confessed to Annie that it was more because Mamie was "*his* daughter" than because of Mamie herself that she felt so bound to her. "I must own that, though I *love* her as much as ever, I feel that she has shown, and *does* show, so little consideration for me, that . . . I sometimes get so angry that I think I will make up my mind to think only of myself! and insist on breaking off and going my own way."

In 1886, Georgina was writing about Mamie to Alfred: "She seems to have quite 'cast her lot' with that clergyman and his wife with whom she has been staying constantly for 8 years. We are all dreadfully sorry . . . and I must say we have a very bad opinion (and with reason I know) of the people with whom she lives. I know she spent all her money upon them and upon his church wherever it may be. She is constantly moving about, and has no settled living anywhere . . . Mamie is of course, entirely her own mistress, and has a right to choose her own way of living. Kate and I have both remonstrated with her many times. But we can do no more, she chooses this life and prefers it, and I can only hope that she may continue to get satisfaction from it . . ."

By the mid-nineties, the situation had grown more ominous. Mamie's always questionable health had taken a severe turn for the worse, and her sister and aunt were very concerned. In early 1896, she went into a decline and Georgina and Kate were traveling to Manchester every three weeks to be with her, "and, of course, are always prepared to go oftener, when necessary, or at an hour's notice at any time." "She was always dearly beloved whenever she came to see us," Georgina wrote to Plorn's wife, Connie, "and stayed with us on special occasions but she had given up all her family and friends for those people whom she had taken to live with her—Mr. Hargreaves is a most unworthy person in every way—and it was always amazing to me that she could keep up this strong feeling of regard and affection for him to the very end of her life. Mrs. Hargreaves has kept true and devoted in her attentions to Mamie during her long illness, and Kitty and I were very grateful to her—I don't know what we could have done without her help . . . Kitty and I had been staying close by for some time—and finally were always in her room." And then, to Plorn himself: "She became gradually past hope—and—at the last Kitty and I went and stayed with her—and remained with her until she died—on the day our poor dear Charley was buried!!"

Even through the decades with the Hargreaveses, Mamie had gone on working to honor and celebrate her father's name. She did a little writing for Charley's *All the Year Round*—articles and even some fiction—and then in the late seventies she and Georgina collaborated to produce three volumes of her father's letters, heavily sanitized but very successful with the public, who until then only had access to those Forster had printed in his biography. (The letters were published by Charley's printing firm, and there were unpleasant financial disagreements among them all.) To Georgina, the letters constituted "a wonderful book—like a new one from the dear dead Hand."

As we have seen, Mamie had finished working on her hagiographic memoir just before her death, but a decade earlier she had published an odd book called *Charles Dickens: By His Eldest Daughter*, a biography written expressly for the young. "If the reading of this little book be the means of making any boys and girls love and venerate the Man—before they can know and love and venerate the Author and the Genius—I shall have accomplished my task with a thankful and a grateful heart."

The basic material is essentially a retelling of the life as we know it from Forster, with a few personal remarks thrown in. It pretends to be objective—she herself is always "his daughter" and Catherine is "Mrs. Dickens," never "my mother"— but it's actually an unmediated outburst of hero-worship and glorification. About Dickens and the blacking factory: "It is touching to see how unselfishly the poor little fellow bore his degraded life, and how unsoured his beautiful nature came out from the trials of that sad time." We hear of "the very brightness and uprightness of his character." We learn that even "in his wildest spirits, he was always considerate of the feelings of others, and never did a thing to hurt or wound his schoolfellow." As for his looks, even when he grew old and his face was lined and worn, "It was still the most beautiful and lovable of all faces in the world." This is not an objective biographer at work but a woman in love.

In a long rhapsodic passage, Mamie evokes her childhood:

There never could have been such parties as those Twelfth Night parties. Never such magic lanterns as those shown by him. Never such conjuring as his: when dressed as a magician, he would make the children scream with laughter . . . Never such suppers as those when he cut up the great Twelfth-cake, and distributed the bonbons and crackers, and waited upon the children like some good fairy, paying attention to all, and making the little cheeks blush, and the eyes sparkle with pleasure, at some kind or funny remark. And then, when he got his little daughters to teach him and a friend the polka, what practices there were before *the* party! . . . And then, when the night of the party came, and the little girls "stood up" to dance with their pupil, what wild beatings of two little hearts, what triumph!

This is the authentic voice of a writer gripped by passionate memory, not only of her father but of her childhood. It would seem that Mamie Dickens never really got beyond that childhood. First, she prolonged it by staying unmarried and living at home with Dickens as an indulged girl into her thirties. After 1870 and his death, she never found anything in life to compare to what was gone. In *My Father as I Recall Him*, she stated it clearly: "My love for my father has never been touched or approached by any other love. I hold him in my heart of hearts as a man apart from all other men, as one apart from all other beings." That turned out not to be a successful recipe for a healthy and satisfying life as an adult.

KATE

K ATE COLLINS was over thirty when her father died. She was still tied to her increasingly ill husband, Charlie, and living without steady income. And although she was improving as an artist, her responsibilities to Charlie took up most of her time as well as undermining her own health—and now she had no Gad's Hill to retire to; she had lost both the person she was closest to and the haven he provided.

At last, in 1873, Charlie died, nursed fanatically by Kate to the final moments. She gave up their little house and moved in with Mamie, Georgina, and Henry, storing most of her possessions in a warehouse that burned down, destroying, among other things, all her father's letters to her and most of her own early artwork. Her health and her spirits revived, however, and she began to create a new life for herself. At least two men proposed marriage to her—Val Prinsep, and another young artist, Fred Walker, with whom she had for some time enjoyed a warm friendship: long walks, coffee in a café on the Embankment. But she was already falling in love with Carlo Perugini, a good-looking, hardworking, and altogether pleasing young artist who was part of her circle—he was a protégé of Lord Leighton's, who for

Kate in the early 1870s

many years employed him as a model and studio assistant. Carlo had been born in Italy but had become a British national, his parents having moved to England when he was eight. He was exactly Kate's age.

Everybody approved of Carlo Perugini. Georgina, reporting to Annie Fields, describes him as "a most sensible, good, honourable and upright man, and *decidedly* attached to Kate. Every one likes him—he is so *perfectly* unaffected, simple and straightforward." He would be, she concludes, a "good and tender guardian [of her] future life and happiness." And the highest praise Georgina could bestow: Dickens himself would have been delighted with this new son-in-law. "This blessed change in her existence would have greatly eased and brightened *him*, I know—and he would have much liked her Husband who I know would have appreciated and loved *him*."

Kate and Carlo were married on June 4, 1874, barely a year after Charlie's death, in almost unseemly haste and very privately. Catherine was not invited, having been told that because they did not want Carlo's parents in attendance, they could not in fairness have her—a lame and hurtful excuse: This was the second of Kate's weddings from which her mother was excluded. Her oldest brother, Charley, being abroad, Frank, back on leave from India, gave Kate away, in the presence of only Mamie, Georgina, Henry, and Millais.

Lucinda Hawksley, working on her invaluable *Katey*, made an extraordinary discovery while doing research at the Family Records Centre in London:

Kate and Carlo married each other twice, within a period of nine months. The first wedding took place on 11 September 1873, barely five months after she had been widowed . . . The wedding was not announced and they did not live together until after their second wedding . . . The most plausible reason for their clandestine marriage is that Kate was, or thought she was, pregnant.

This wedding is never mentioned by Kate or anyone else; it would certainly have provoked an ugly scandal if it had come to light. It was bad enough that she waited only a year after her first husband's death to marry publicly.

Now began the long and mostly sunny period of Kate's middle years. Not only was she happily married to a man who adored her, but her career was blossoming as well: Her paintings were beginning to sell, and by 1877 her work was being accepted by the Royal Academy for its annual exhibitions. The greatest joy of these years was the birth of the couple's one child, Leonard Ralph Dickens Perugini, called Dickie, at the very close of 1875. Kate had been highly anxious about the birth (she was thirty-six), and it turned out to be a long and difficult one, but the baby was physically per-

The Flower Merchant, *by Kate Dickens Perugini*

fect and was adored by its parents and the entire Dickens family. Then, at the age of seven months, Dickie suffered a sudden and devastating illness (the doctor diagnosed it as a bowel inflammation), and in two days was dead. Again, Georgina's letter to Annie Fields tells the story: "I cannot tell you what grief it is to Katey . . . Her love for the child was a revelation to *herself*, of a power of loving she did not know she had in her . . . [Dickie was a] fine, *noble* engaging creature—with the sweetest nature—so patient in his suffering! I think he was one of those children who are not *meant* to live. He looks so pretty in Death."

In the late seventies Kate embarked on what would prove to be the most lucrative aspect of her career, painting commissioned portraits of children, but she also branched out in various directions, at times taking advantage of her Dickens name by painting scenes from her father's novels, beginning with "Little Nell" for the Royal Academy, and making five woodcuts to illustrate *The Charles Dickens Birthday Book*. In 1886 she was named a professional member of the prestigious Society of Lady Artists (later the Society of Women Artists), and although Carlo was considered the more serious artist—he usually worked on a larger scale—most of the Peruginis' income came from Kate. One can see why. Her portraits of children are scrupulously painted, their subjects flattered, perhaps, but not fulsomely so (although one is grateful that something called "There's a Sweet Little Cherub That Sits Up Aloft" has been lost). She's expert with flowers and clothing—literal, but occasionally veering in the direction of Renoir. All in all, she's an accomplished and pleasing artist. Carlo's work is closer to the Pre-Raphaelites, with whom he was always identified, and often with classical subjects, yet a straightforward picture of Kate (one of many that he painted) is a ravishing traditional portrait of a young-ish, handsome, composed, and slightly amused woman.

Kate was criticized for being too far under the influence of her mentor, Millais; a fierce review to that effect by George Bernard Shaw led to a long, intense correspondence between the two of them. Hawksley points out how revealing her letters to Shaw are of her personality—and temper. "Nothing at this moment," she writes to him, "could afford me such supreme satisfaction as to see you writhe in anguish." Her letters, Hawksley concludes, "reveal a woman who is used to using her charms to get what she wants—and who usually succeeds."

Hawksley also quotes in full a letter she calls, with only slight exaggeration, "superbly witty and clever."

Dear Mr. Bernard Shaw, I have been very busy, very poorly and in such low spirits that art & literature—the world—and every body and every thing in it—even Socialism—have all seemed to me but "vanity and vexation of spirit." To-day I am a little better, so I will try to answer your letter, which with the article you so kindly sent me, I read with a great deal of interest,—and not a little amusement. You dont [*sic*] in the least frighten me by describing yourself as a Socialist, although I confess I have very vague ideas as to what Socialism really means.

I take a Socialist to be a kind of Radical philanthropist, who wishes to do all the good he can in the world, but who in so doing would also like to take away from the lives of people all that makes life beautiful and worth having—and who would reduce the world at last to as dull a level as—Gower Street on a cold spring day, with dust flying and cold pale yellow oranges being cried and sold! I also imagine a Socialist (for some inscrutable reason of his own) to have rather ungracious manners and to wear creaky boots, but no doubt I am wrong. The only Socialist I know is indeed very unlike this, he has a pretty house, gives charming dinners—and rumour has it, that he rides in the Row every morning on a very handsome horse—but I suppose my Socialist has not the courage of his opinions—or he would live on a crust, would he not? and cut up his horse into mincemeat to divide among his poorer friends?

But as I have already said, I have vague ideas on the subject—I should like to see a real thorough going young Socialist in the flesh, I would therefore repeat my invitation to you—only of one thing I am most horribly afraid. I am afraid of boring people—I consider it should be a punishable crime to bore anyone, and as you seem to think it would bore you to come and see me, I have nothing for it, although I regret it very much, but to beg you to stay away. Your startling assertion that you hate all artists is a little sweeping is it not for even a Socialist to affirm? I imagined a Socialist was a very large minded individual indeed—but again I fear I have been wrong in my estimation of him, but in this case I cannot be expected to agree with you. My husband is an artist, my father was one—and although a humble wretched little painter I try to be one myself. I therefore cannot hate artists—although I do not think art will save the world—but will Socialism? Both have some good in them surely—and might ought rather to walk hand in hand—doing all the good they can together—than sulk off separately and make themselves disagreeable.

Yrs very sincerely
Kate Perugini

Here we see her flirtatious, provocative, clever, and charming—the Katey Dickens (and Kate Perugini) everyone adored. No wonder she was her father's favorite.

Kate's friendship with Shaw deepened and survived for

many years—at times even causing friction between her and Carlo. It was to Shaw that she wrote, "If you could make the public understand that my father was not a joyous, jocund gentleman walking around the world with a plum pudding and a bowl of punch, you would greatly oblige me." And when she faced the important decision about how to dispose of her father's letters to her mother—which, just before Catherine died, she had entrusted to Kate—after endless deliberation she accepted his advice and gave them to the British Museum rather than destroy them. (Catherine had wanted them preserved to prove to the world that at one time Charles had loved her.) Although she grew closer to her mother in the years after Dickens's death and spent a good deal of time with her, they were never close the way Catherine had been with Charley, Sydney, Henry, and Plorn—possibly because Kate could never really overcome her guilt at having once turned her back on her mother.

Shaw was only one of the many men and women to whom Kate became attached in the latter half of her very long life. Her closest friend of all remained Anny Thackeray Ritchie (and later Anny's daughter, Hester, who touchingly asked permission to call her "Aunt Kitty"). J. M. Barrie was a particular friend; W. S. Gilbert another; G. K. Chesterton yet another. Henry James was less close but also part of her life. (She read *The Aspern Papers* avidly but with some distress, given the uncomfortable parallels between its story and her own situation.) Over the decades she left her home less and less frequently, partly because, even apart from his habitual shyness, Carlo was increasingly unwell and found it difficult to go out. But the world came to her—a constant stream of guests at tea-time and at her Sunday at-homes.

In fact, despite her being more and more home-bound, Kate's circle expanded in the early years of the twentieth century as she became involved with the doings of the Dickens Fellowship, attending (and dominating) its meetings as long as she was able to go out, and entertaining members at home when she couldn't; she was its president for many years. During World War I, she and Anny urged people to send copies of their fathers' books to soldiers at the front.

W. M. THACKERAY   CHARLES DICKENS

AN APPEAL

GREAT Public ! You who love to read our fathers,
With memory of whom our work to-day is done ;
Be generous as they ; and for our Heroes
Give—as these writers gave their tears and fun.

*   *   *   *   *   *

We ask no more than all that you can spare,
And crave forgiveness if we greatly dare.

ANNE ISABELLA RITCHIE
KATE PERUGINI

HYDE PARK HOUSE
ALBERT GATE, S.W.   22nd November, 1916

The poetry is all too typical of the verse that Kate turned out by the cartload during these years. A typical effusion (about her loyal maid):

Our Ellen is thoughtful though she is gay
Her spirit is lively and clever
She makes her friends happy and through the day
No grumble is heard from her ever!

She also wrote articles—first for Charley's *All the Year Round*, later for other journals, often on subjects related to her father. And she began a book about her parents, though, after years of working on it, she abandoned it without showing it to a publisher and burned the only copy of the manuscript. "I only told the half-truth about my father," she said, "and a half-truth is worse than a lie."

Her connections to the family remained intense, although her relationship with Mamie weakened after her marriage to Carlo and as Mamie's life grew odder. She was an inconsistent correspondent but a lively one when she remembered to write, and there are fond letters to the overseas brothers. She stayed involved with the lives of Charley's many daughters, trying to help them find work as typists for her writer friends. As time passed and the ten-year gap between her and Henry grew less important, she grew closer and closer to him, although there was always a coolness toward Henry's wife, partly due to Marie's Catholicism. In her very old age, her mind slipping away, Kate was convinced that Marie was somehow going to give her a Catholic burial—something that neither Henry (who hadn't converted to his wife's religion) or for that matter the Catholic Church would ever have countenanced.

Her innermost circle, however, was shrinking dramatically, first when in 1917 her Aunt Georgie, whom she had been devotedly nursing, died following severe dementia—a sad ending for that formidable person; and a year later when Carlo died of the angina that had plagued him for many years. They had enjoyed more than forty years of a generous if occasionally ruffled marriage, surviving the loss of their adored baby and the eternal financial problems that never ceased to badger them. (Fortunately, at about this time a Mr. Wagg—father of two of Kate's friends—left her in his will an annuity of £300 a year as a token of gratitude to Dickens, of whom he was a lifetime passionate admirer. "I've come into a fortune!" she exclaimed to a friend. Her financial anxieties were resolved forever.) A year after Carlo's death she lost Anny Ritchie.

She was still attracting new admirers, though, chief among them T. P. O'Connor, who was, among other things, the "Father of the House of Commons"—that is, the member who in his day had served the longest consecutive time: forty-nine years. (He was succeeded in this distinction by David Lloyd George and, later, Winston Churchill.) He was also the first president of the British Board of Film Censors. O'Connor was nine years younger than Kate, but he admired and loved her from the time they met, around 1911, until her death, calling on her regularly until his rheumatism prevented him from climbing her stairs; writing to her; sending flowers, candy, even a gramophone. And birthday telegrams: "My best wishes and fond love my dearest sweetheart."

As was true of her father, her mood swings were pronounced. At times she was still full of fun and ginger, teasing and flirting. (And smoking!) At other times, she was seriously depressed, particularly—again, like her father—when the weather was bleak and it was dark outside. She was,

Gladys Storey tells us, "seldom if ever offended for she possessed deep and wide understanding, and her abounding sense of humor enabled her to see the funny side of most things." "Once, but *never* twice!" was a favorite expression when asked to do things she had no interest in doing, and "Laugh it to scorn!" was her preferred way of reacting to those who challenged her opinions. She was always outspoken. "I'm not a lady, you know, I'm too much of a socialist to be a lady. My father was not a gentleman—he was far too mixed to be a gentleman. My mother was a lady born and by Education also my grandfather." (About Marie: "She's not a lady but thinks she is.")

She very much feared dying—no doubt in part a reflection of her tremendous zest for living. "Her thoughts concerning the next world were uncertain," wrote Storey. "Some years previously, when a clergyman called to see her and talked about the joys awaiting us in Heaven, she looked at him and said, 'How do you know?' And yet, when she was feeling particularly depressed and ill, she would clasp her hands in supplication and say, 'Dear God, it would be very kind of you to help me.'"

Her mind began to wander, she grew confused, and as she became more and more terrified of death she became convinced that she *would* die if she went to sleep in her bed. (Hawksley: "She seemed truly to believe that, as long as she avoided her bed, she really would be able to cheat death out of claiming her.") Instead, she would sleep in her armchair, or roam around her rooms through the nights. She would lie for hours in a coma-like sleep during the days. One night her maids moved her into her bed, and by morning she was gone, only a few months short of her ninetieth birthday.

The London *Times* wrote in its obituary:

From her early childhood she won the hearts of all who knew her . . . Mrs. Perugini inherited her father's characteristics of wit, whimsicality, common sense in all things, and a broad outlook on life and humanity. She was a brilliant but at the same time thoughtful talker. Her conversation was full of fun, her eyes seemed to sparkle in the enjoyment of it, her radiant and honest smile lighting up her beautiful face . . . She was a lovable woman most fascinating in manner, with a sense of humour that she must have inherited from her father, an artist to the tips of her fingers, ever loyal to her friends and with a wonderful patience in the physical discomfort of her later years. It is given to few people to make as many loyal and loving friends as she did, and to leave such kindly memories behind her as she will to those who survive her.

Among those closest to her in her later years was her beloved maid Ellen, who a year after Kate's death said, "I never thought I could still be missing her after all these months, I loved her so." And six months after that: "I still miss and miss the little soul. I don't think there will ever be another like her."

FRANK

Frank's seven-year career in India, where according to Georgina he had an excellent record, ended when in 1871 he returned to England for the standard six-month leave. His long-anticipated visit, however, proved a disappointment, although he was attractive in manner and in looks—a handsome young man with a golden mustache. Georgina wrote to Annie Fields, "He seems affectionate and pleased to see us when we do, but I don't think he cares much about any one." There is no mention of romantic attachments in India. His leave coincided with the final disposition of his father's will, and Frank came into his substantial inheritance—which he quickly and carelessly dissipated, at one point failing to keep an important appointment with Frederic Ouvry, now his own solicitor. "I hope," Georgina went on, "that he had merely forgotten." It is during this period that he most seriously displeased his aunt over the matter of repurchasing his father's miniature chalet after Charley had sold it. "It is a sad disappointment to find so many unworthy sons of their great Father, isn't it!"

When his leave was up, he simply failed to go back to his regiment in India, throwing away his army career. Much of his money was soon lost in a failed speculation in indigo; the rest he seems to have squandered. "I know very little of Frank," Georgina told Ouvry, "and all that I know is most sad and hopeless . . . What he intends to do, I have not the faintest idea. It seems of no use making any effort to help him. Both his sisters have tried and so have I to put him in the way of getting employment—but it is in vain. He has appointments made for him with men who seem likely and willing to be of use to him—and he does not keep them. So it all ends in his giving offence—and bringing discredit on those who endeavour to do him good. I think he is mad—I really do." Henry in his *Recollections* refers sympathetically to "Frank, whom I always considered the cleverest and best read of us all, in spite of a very quick temper and strange oddities of manner." What oddities, Sir Henry? Sexual, perhaps? We have no way of knowing, but Frank's entire life suggests complicated, unhappy—and unresolved—problems.

As Arthur Adrian writes in his book on Georgina,

Penniless, he disappeared. After a search of some months, Georgina and Mamie located him "very miserable and very penitent and anxious to do *any* work to begin *life* again." Mamie appealed to a number of their father's friends for help. To one of them in Philadelphia she wrote that Frank had never asked Dickens for a penny or given him any anxiety after leaving for India. Even now, though he had wasted his own money foolishly, he had taken nothing that did not belong to him. "He is now thirty—clever, well educated, a gentleman. He is fully alive to his folly & is sincerely grieved & ashamed to have come to us for help."

Dickens commanding
his men, Fort Pitt,
c. 1885

Inspector F. J. Dickens and North-West Mounted Police personnel

The family's efforts at last proved successful. Lord Frederick Dufferin, recently appointed the third Governor-General of Canada, was a friend, and was prevailed upon to procure for Frank an appointment to the North-West Mounted Police, which allowed him to resume the active outdoor life he had enjoyed in India. Kate, along with Mamie, Harry, and the two boys in Australia, chipped in to give Frank a good start in his new life. (These loans were never repaid.) "We all went to see him off at the station," Georgina wrote to Annie. "Harry went with him to Liverpool, and said he was very much 'cut up' at last—but he was *most* anxious and thankful to go. I cannot tell you what a relief it is to have got this place for him."

Frank's years in Canada were as filled with contradictions and disappointments as his earlier life. Things did not begin well—he was late (not through his own fault) in getting to his first posting, at Winnipeg. A negative report on him, filed in these first days of his service, impeded his progress ("A very poor officer of no promise. Physically weak in constitution, his habits not affording good example." What habits were those?), yet he was eventually promoted from sub-inspector to inspector.

In the 1870s, the government's control of the Northwest Territories over various groups of rebellious and aggressive Indians and renegades was still tenuous. For close to twelve years Frank worked under bleak circumstances in the grim outposts to which the Mounties were consigned, spread across Manitoba, Alberta, and Saskatchewan. "He chased whiskey smugglers, Indians, outlaws and fugitives across the Canadian prairies," wrote the historian Carol McLeod. "In summer he endured ravenous mosquitoes and scorching heat and in winter braved temperatures of ‾50° F." During all that time he had no leave or break in his duties, and his physical condition, never robust, was steadily going downhill—he had grown increasingly deaf, exacerbating his already pronounced tendency to self-imposed isolation. One recent commentator has said of him, "He preferred to go on solitary hikes across the prairies—a small, moody, heavily bearded man with the two companions who never goaded him, an Irish retriever and a favourite shotgun." His one vice, apparently, was liquor—it is mentioned in his file. When encouraged to write about his experiences, given that he was the son of a great writer, he answered, "I shall write one book. Its subject shall be the prohibition dry North West Territories and its title—Forty years Without Beer." His biographer, David J. Carter, in his book *Inspector F. J. Dickens of the North-West Mounted Police*—published as recently as 2003—includes the following positive observations in a list he calls "Summation":

Dickens did not have any "social disease" such as afflicted a considerable number of the NWMP.

Dickens did not desert the NWMP as did a number of his contemporaries.

Dickens was not known to "consort" with aboriginal women as did quite a number of his contemporaries.

Frank's reputation was generally favorable in the immediate aftermath of his service, particularly locally in the Territories; then harshly unfavorable for an extended period, especially in the *Dictionary of Canadian Biography*, which concludes "Francis Dickens made a definite, if negative, impact on the Canadian west. He was partly responsible for the serious deterioration in relations between the NWMP and the Blackfoot in the 1880s. His misadventures also contributed to the strong prejudice against English officers that existed in the mounted police in the late 19th century." More recently, he has made a comeback, particularly in regard to the incident with which he has been most closely associated: the forced retreat of the Mounties from Fort Pitt, a small trading post on the Saskatchewan River, in 1885. The *Dictionary* recounts the story baldly:

After the opening of hostilities at Frog Lake (Alta) on 2 April 1885, some 28 civilians sought refuge in Fort Pitt. Eleven days later Big Bear [a Cree chief, with whom Dickens was on relatively amicable terms] appeared and demanded the surrender of the fort. Dickens refused and two days of negotiations followed which came to an end when a scouting party of three policemen stumbled

into the Cree camp. In the ensuing gun-fight one consta-
ble was killed, a second was wounded, and the third was
taken prisoner. At this point the civilians in the fort decided to give themselves up to Big Bear because Fort Pitt
was poorly sited for defense and lacked an internal water
supply. Dickens then decided to abandon the post and
retreat down-river to Battleford. A scow was hastily con-
structed and after six days Dickens and his men reached
safety.

The actual retreat was far more difficult and harrowing than
this account would suggest. The fort was indefensible and
Frank was left with twenty able-bodied men in uniform under
his command, plus half a dozen civilians, mostly women and
children. The weather was severe, and the several hundred
hostiles were threatening. David Carter describes the flight
from the fort:

> It was a rough trip. Huge blocks of ice crashed continu-
> ally into the sides of the scow and it began to fill with
> water as the wind whipped waves over the gunwales. The
> river was three hundred yards wide and the current was
> swift. Some of the more playful Indians could not resist
> loosing a few rifle shots at the labouring boat and all
> hands were too busy keeping afloat to answer the fire.
>
> For six days, the Mounties fought ice, current and
> gale, bailing furiously, as they pushed the leaky scow
> downstream to Battleford. Their soaked clothing froze
> to their bodies and the water ruined some of their food
> and ammunition. Finally they stumbled ashore before
> the stockade of the headquarters of the Northern dis-

trict, which was still under siege, but was safe. A Mountie band played them into the enclosure, they were warmed and fed and told that they had done all that could have been expected of them.

At the time and on the spot, Dickens was much praised for having managed the evacuation of Fort Pitt so bravely and successfully. The Battleford newspaper wrote on May 18, "Let us here do justice to the men who have distinguished themselves in this North-Western campaign. First, let us mention Inspector Dickens, whose gallant defense of Fort Pitt saved the police from destruction at the hands of a large body of Indians."

But by now it was clear that Frank's life as a Mountie was at an end. He was exhausted and weak, and his hearing so impaired that it was hard for him to carry out his duties. Traveling to Ottawa, he resigned from the force on February 16, 1886, and after considerable maneuvering and negotiation, accepted a "retiring gratuity of one year's pay." Waiting for this money to arrive, and uncertain what to do next with his life (he was only forty-two), he accepted the invitation of an American he had recently befriended in Toronto, Dr. A. W. Jamieson, to return with him to his home in Moline, Illinois, with the idea of giving public lectures about his life as a Mountie and readings from his father's works. On May 27 the two men arrived at the Jamieson farm.

Decades later, Jamieson's daughter, Louise Jamieson Alsterlund, described what happened two weeks after that, on June 11, when Frank was dining at the home of the editor of the Moline *Republican* before addressing the Friday Club on one of the dramatic episodes of his life as a policeman:

While at the table Captain Dickens took a drink of iced water and almost immediately appeared much distressed. Noticing this, after a moment, father assisted him to rise and conducted him through the library into the parlor. The Captain said, with some effort, "It was the water; when I drank it I felt as if I had been stabbed." He was placed in a reclining chair, his clothing loosened and every possible attention given him. After a short time he declared he was resting easier and begged that the dinner go on without interruption. Thinking he would feel better if left alone most of the party returned to the table. In a few moments a great change in the Captain occurred. The fan fell from his hands; his fingers worked convulsively and he seemed struggling for breath. For the first time alarm was felt as to the result. Stimulants were quickly given and unremitting efforts made to restore respiration, but he gave little sign of reviving. He was then lifted from the reclining chair and carried to bed in an adjoining room and vigorous efforts renewed to restore life, but without result, save one sigh. He was dead. Dr. Davidson had been called and both doctors united in saying the cause of death was paralysis of the heart, precipitated perhaps by the small amount of cold water he drank. It was about 6:10 when the first shock came, and all was over within fifteen minutes.

Charley, notified by telegram, requested that his brother's body be buried in Moline, and since Frank had no money with him (his $1,000 gratuity check had not yet arrived), the people of the town banded together to pay for his well-attended funeral and burial. Two years later, Charley and Bessie came to Moline (he was on a reading tour of America) and visited the grave. A tombstone was erected for which Bessie chose the biblical verse "Take ye heed, watch and pray; for ye know not when the time is. Mark 13, v.33."

Today, there are *two* headstones over Frank's grave in the Moline cemetery. In 2002 a group of both active and retired Mounties, together with some interested civilians, arranged to erect the second one—perhaps to make amends for the RCMP's dismissive attitude toward him during and after his years of service.

In 1942, more than half a century after his death, Mrs. Alsterlund characterized Frank this way: "I was but a young girl then but I have a distinct recollection of him—a quiet unassuming man . . . As he sat one day in our living room with one of his father's works in his hand he said to my

The two headstones at the grave of Frank Dickens,
Moline, Illinois

Mother, 'I'm glad my father never wrote anything that was harmful for young or old to read.'" He had never ceased venerating Charles, and treasured the few Dickens relics he possessed. His father's gold watch had been left behind in the hurried retreat from Fort Pitt, but afterward it was retrieved. Still later, he hocked it.

ALFRED

ALFRED WAS TWENTY-FOUR when his father died. The shock was intense—he had no idea that Dickens's health was so seriously impaired. On August 11, 1870, he wrote to Mr. Rusden:

I cannot tell you what an awful blow it has been to me: coming as it did so awfully unexpectedly and suddenly. I do not think I properly realized the full extent of my loss till yesterday when my home letters came, and then all hope of some mistake or contradiction vanished. It is very hard to think that I shall never see him again, and that he who was so good, so gentle with us all has passed away . . .

There is but one unfortunate incident in our dear father's life, and that was his separation from our mother. As people will doubtless talk about this, may I ask you to state the facts properly for myself & Plorn, should they be misrepresented. When the separation took place, it made no difference in our feelings towards them: we children always loved them both equally, having free intercourse with both, as of old: while not one word of the subject *ever* passed from the lips of either father or mother. Of the causes which led to this unfortunate event, we know no more than the rest of the world. Our dear mother has suffered very much. My brother's wife [Bessie] in her letter says "Poor dear she is better than I dared to hope she would be, and I am sure that in a little time she will be more settled, and even happier than she has been for years, for she says what is true that she has already lived 12 years of widowhood, and now she feels that there is nobody nearer to him than she is."

My heart is too full to write on any other subject but this today.

Characteristically, he is concerned for his younger brother Plorn, and in the same spirit of generosity he writes to Ouvry asking whether Georgina and Mamie need financial help. (Touched, Georgina comments that although she had "no need to accept, thank God!" she "can't help remarking that he is the only one (except Harry) to whom it seems to have occurred that Mamie and I have had some little difficulty to go through in making our great change." (Actually, Georgina and Mamie had both come into considerable funds from Dickens's will—larger than Alfred's share.)

Alfred's own inheritance seems to have been spent and lost in acquiring a sheep station of his own. He also at this time tried and failed to become a magistrate. Moving from the outback to Melbourne, he went to work with the London and Australia Agency Corporation Limited in their wool warehouses and offices, and seems to have prospered—his early business experience in London came into useful play here, combined with his hands-on experience with sheep.

In 1873 he made a highly suitable marriage, to Miss Jessie Devlin, whose father was a master mariner. (He gave his own and his father's "rank or profession" as "Gentleman.") Georgina writes to Annie Fields, "We know all about the young lady—as she is a connection of some kind neighbours of ours at Gad's Hill. So it is all right in *that* way. Alfred, of course, says she is 'beautiful and accomplished,' and we hear, from other sources, that she is a very nice pretty girl who is likely to make him a good wife . . . And it is a great comfort to us to think that as he is obliged to spend so much of his life in that distant colony he should be going to make a *home* there, to take away the feeling of exile which one cannot [help] having for young men who have to work so far from home." And she confirms that Alfred is doing well financially, so that there is "nothing improvident in his taking this important step in life." Mamie, too, is pleased when she receives a "nice letter from her new sister-in-law," which strengthened her conviction that this marriage was "the greatest blessing to both." Jessie's photograph reassures her that the bride is "very good and pretty—a perfectly nice, unaffected girl."

Unfortunately, the business Alfred was working for suffered disaster, first legal and then financial, and in 1874 went into liquidation. He had been, some months earlier, on a business trip to the small town of Hamilton in the Western District of Victoria. (The railroad didn't arrive there until three years later; its population today is about 10,000, and it likes to think of itself as the Wool Capital of the World.) Soon, he entered into partnership with Hamilton's auctioneer and stock and station agent, and bought a large house with nine rooms and a garden setting for Jessie and himself and their baby daughter, Kathleen. (A second daughter, Violet, would be born soon after the family's arrival in Hamilton.) The young couple certainly had sufficient funds, for they were able to furnish their new home lavishly in the style of the day, with oil paintings, Wedgwood statuettes, a piano, and "a splendid mahogany side board."

Quickly they were welcomed into the social life of the community (he was, to begin with, a son of the great Charles Dickens), taking their place in both the town's church life and its sporting life—Alfred was an excellent cricketer (honorary secretary of the Cricket Association) and horseman (member of the Racing Club). He was, as well, a member of the Whist Club and the honorary treasurer of the Hamilton Hospital and one of the trustees of the Hamilton Savings Bank. In other words, he was now a prosperous and popular still-young man in a flourishing town—and a happy husband and father.

It all came crashing down on December 14, 1878, when Jessie was killed in an accident while driving through the streets in her pony carriage.

The local newspaper reflects the town's distress: "It can be safely asserted that no lady was more popular, and that when the news arrived that Mrs Dickens was dead, many could scarcely realise the fact. Only a few, short hours previously she had been seen driving about in her well-known pony carriage, in the full enjoyment of health, youth, and beauty." The ponies—"a spirited pair"—had "bolted down the street at a fearful rate," and Jessie, trying to help the boy who was driving, grabbed at the reins. She may have pulled at the wrong one; the carriage ran into a gutter and flung her out, "her head landing with violence on the metalled road." She was insensible when she was carried to the doctor, who "saw at once that no human skill could be of any avail as the skull had been fractured." Three hours later she was dead.

Alfred was undone. Georgina wrote to Annie Fields that he had sent the family in England "a perfectly heartbroken and heart *breaking* letter, all the more touching from its manly resignation and truly religious tone." He stayed on in Hamilton for another three years, his little girls, aged four and two when their mother died, under the care of Jessie's closest friend, Polly McLellan, who became their beloved Aunt Polly. Not surprisingly, however, Alfred eventually decided to leave the place of which his memories were so unhappy. He and his auctioneer partner amicably dissolved their business, and Alfred moved back to Melbourne, where he and Plorn, who had also returned there, joined forces to launch a new stock and station agency.

His departure from Hamilton was marked by a series of farewell events that demonstrate the respect and affection with which he was held there, in particular a banquet at which a toast "alluded to his genial social qualities"—a toast that "was received with an amount of enthusiasm that has seldom been witnessed." His household goods having been successfully auctioned off, he left for Melbourne in September 1882.

"Any stranger visiting the Hamilton Station on Tuesday," reported the *Spectator*,

> just as the train was about to leave for Melbourne, would quickly have become aware that something out of the common was occurring, there being so numerous a gathering of ladies and gentlemen on the platform. The cause of the muster was the departure of Mr A.T. Dickens,

whose friends had attended to bid him farewell. There was an attempt at cheering, but it was only an attempt, so many being sincerely sorry at having to part with a friend who, at the social board and on all occasions, had been looked upon by them "as a real jolly good fellow."

The brothers' new enterprise was heralded in *The Australasian*: "How the Dickens can I put it? Best plainly. Two sons of Charles Dickens are about to commence business as station agents in Melbourne. One of them (Alfred Tennyson) is well known in Victoria. With the other, (Plorn in his father's correspondence) we are perhaps not so familiar. Surely their father's sons deserve well of us, and the rest of the human race, and let them have their deserts. I wish I had twenty stations for them to sell." The arrangement did not last long, however; in 1883, Plorn quit Melbourne to return to his life in the outback.

The following years in Alfred's life are obscure—he was rarely mentioned in the local newspapers. He went on managing E.B.L. Dickens and Company for some while, presumably benefiting from a boom economy—so much so that in 1888, at the age of forty-three, he married again, to an Emile (or Emily) Rebecca Riley, who was twenty-four. Very little is known about her, and in later years he rarely mentioned her; the assumption has been that it was not a happy marriage. Oddly, Alfred's two daughters went on living with "Aunt Polly," in a different area of Melbourne from the one in which their father and his new wife were now residing. And within a few years, the economic bubble burst: Businesses were going under, banks were failing. In 1891, to supplement his income, Alfred began giving public lectures about his father, punctuated with readings from his works. Years earlier, in Hamilton, he had done this on a single occasion, to benefit a charity.

Although money for entertainment was now scarce, the readings went forward, well received by the press. *The Sydney Morning Herald*, for instance, reported that "considering the wretchedly wet evening the audience was large, most of the seats in the hall being filled. The lecture proved to be a real treat, for the lecturer, in addition to possessing a good voice, delivery and address, enjoys the advantage of being able to invest his subject with the charm of close personal experience, instead of the mere book knowledge with which other lecturers on the great novelist have to rest."

Inevitably, the station-agent business ceased to exist, and for a while Alfred was listed in the Directory as a financial agent (whatever that was). Later, he offered several versions of what had gone wrong with his finances: He was unfortunate in his investments; he lost almost everything when a disease destroyed his flocks of sheep, worth $100,000. Some money came in from funds dispersed to Mamie's living siblings following her death in 1896. Alfred managed to get by, though never again with conspicuous success, and by 1908, his daughters were earning their own livings—Violet as a governess away with a family, Kathleen teaching piano and viola and, according to Directory entries, living at the same address as her stepmother. And Alfred went on giving his lectures and readings; the public's fascination with Dickens never waned.

In 1910—he was now sixty-five—he decided to carry his new career to England and America. *The Dickensian* in its June issue announced his coming: "We need hardly say that

Mr. Dickens will meet with a hearty welcome wherever he goes." Another journalist predicted, "Considering the enormous manner in which he has already been booked, his tour will be a very satisfactory one." He would be giving the same kind of lecture that had worked so well in Australia, "personal rather than literary and reminiscent of the novelist's goodness of heart during his fame and prosperity rather than his early boyish struggles."

When Alfred arrived in England after an absence of forty-five years, only two of his siblings were still alive: Kate and Harry. (Aunt Georgie, in her eighties, was frail and unable to attend Alfred's performances, but reported that she had heard that what he had to say was "all very nice.") Relations with Kate and Carlo Perugini were warm, but there was no warmth between Alfred and Harry. In an interview long afterward, Harry suggested that his brother had a serious drinking problem, and there had been ugly difficulties over money. The fissure was so deep that in his *Recollections* Harry skipped over Alfred's visit to England; instead, he had him going directly to America, "quite a stranger to the family from the time he went to Australia."

Alfred lectured "throughout the length and breadth of the British Isles almost without cessation"—sixty-six performances—under considerable physical strain, an unfortunate echo of his father's killing schedule during *his* lecturing years. *The Dickensian* wrote that he attributed his success "to the love and veneration that exists in this country for his father's memory," but goes on to suggest that "those who have heard Mr Alfred Tennyson Dickens need not be told that his modesty prompts such a statement from him, for his own personality, the nature of his lecture, and the remarkably lucid and natural manner he adopts in delivering it assures interest and creates enthusiasm apart from the asset he possesses in being his father's son." The whole thing was a real, and lucrative, success—his first public appearance in London "met with a great reception." He was also gratified at being elected a vice president of the Dickens Fellowship when he attended its annual meeting in Brighton. But after seeing Alfred off at London's Euston Station, on his way to embark for America, *The Dickensian*'s editor expressed considerable concern about the state of his health.

His first stop in America was Boston, which he found "a most delightful place and the people themselves charming." He then proceeded to New York before swinging west as far as Denver. He was a big success in the Midwest, his welcome in St. Louis typical: He addressed the high school, whose students all wore little bouquets of red geraniums in honor of his father, whose favorite flowers they were. There were local excursions involving lunches and dinners and receptions, including one to a spot on the Mississippi where his father had stood looking westward on his first American tour in 1842. Asked whether "it did not make him sad to stand where his father had stood so many years ago," he replied, "Why should it? I am standing in the same place almost every day. I never forget my father for a moment. I feel he is always with me, you know."

During a three-day visit to Cairo, Illinois (he stayed with the mayor), the local newspaper wrote of the official reception that "no affair of the kind ever occurred in Cairo which was so generally attended and so well enjoyed by its citizens and we believe it was equally as well enjoyed and appreciated by Mr Dickens." Wherever he went he was enthusiastically welcomed and applauded—first, of course, as his father's son; more than forty years after Dickens died, he remained a potent and beloved figure in America—but also for his own friendliness and modesty. Alfred was so occupied with lecturing and traveling that he had to refuse flattering invitations (one, for instance, from President Taft) so that "not once from the very inception of the tour did he disappoint

Alfred Dickens with his daughters Kathleen and Violet

an audience." His fees were high—in England, up to three hundred pounds a performance—but the strain on his health was pronounced: Before he left England there had been clear indications that his heart might give way within months.

Returning to New York for a second lecture, he arrived at his hotel, the Astor, on December 30, 1911. The next day he felt so unwell that he was examined by the hotel doctor, who diagnosed indigestion. At midday he collapsed in the lobby, dictated several letters, fell asleep, awoke later in the afternoon, said a few words to his secretary, and fell back dead. Notified by telegram, Kathleen and Violet preferred that his sister, Kate, decide about the funeral arrangements (his alienated second wife was not consulted), and Kate chose to have him buried in New York (the burial paid for by a group of distinguished New Yorkers) rather than have his remains returned to England—or Australia. They lie now in Trinity Church Cemetery in Washington Heights. His pallbearers included Andrew Carnegie and Whitelaw Reid.

There were spontaneous tributes not only in the newspapers but from various Americans he had recently encountered on his travels. The wife of Missouri's governor, for instance, who had spent a day with him on one of his excursions there, found him "so likable and unassuming," and noted "the simplicity of the kindly man"; someone else spoke of his "agreeable and easy manner and his cordial handshake. In private and public he comported himself with true dignity, coupled however with affability."

The New York Times ran an extended obituary on January 3, 1912, over the headline "SON OF DICKENS DIES AT THE ASTOR Tennyson's Namesake Expires There of Acute Indigestion, After a Brief Illness." Quoted in the story, Alfred's American manager confirmed that everyone associated with him during the tour had learned to like "the kindly son of the great novelist," and that Alfred, in turn, had "formed a strong attachment for America and his friends here," going on to report "that in his opinion, America and Australia were the greatest countries in the world," and adding "with that charming humor of his, that it's a pity they are not hitched up together." He also stated that the plan had been for Alfred to continue in America until June, return to England for a second round of performances, and move on to South Africa before returning home to Australia in two years. It is easy to agree with the Melbourne *Argus*'s reflection that "It is to be regretted that just as he was meeting with long deferred successes, he should not live to reap the benefits of his triumphs."

Alfred died just a month short of his father's hundredth birthday. He would have been pleased at the coincidence.

The year after Alfred's death, his two daughters, Violet and Kathleen, traveled to England to visit the relatives they had never met. The visit was a success, Henry remarking in his memoirs that Alfred "left two daughters, who came over to this country some years ago, and remain great favourites with all of us," and one of his daughters remembering them as "charming women," while Mary Lazarus tells us that "this is certainly the impression I had of them in 1951." They had gone back to Australia for a short time following the 1913 trip but then decided to return permanently to England and the only family they had, and where they died in the early 1950s. Violet and Kathleen had been, as Lazarus points out, the last link between Charles Dickens and Australia.

SYDNEY

GEORGINA, via her letters, is our chief source for what happened to Sydney during the short time between his father's death and his own. To Ouvry, Dickens's trusted solicitor who was handling his affairs for him, he had written when his father died, "I feel exceedingly obliged to you for your advice, but no one than myself can better understand the misery of being involved in debt and difficulties." And he presented himself to Georgina herself "very miserably and remorsefully." Although he was still caught up in a skein of debts, she felt sorry for him, and as Dickens's co-executor, helped pay off his creditors from his share of the estate. "We can only hope and trust that he may take a lesson from the awful calamity that has fallen upon him. It is impossible to judge until we see him, what reason there is for hope—or the reverse—about him."

In December, six months after his father's death, he was back in England. "Sydney was here yesterday evening," Georgina wrote to Ouvry, "in a *most* wretched state, poor boy! and full of good intentions—which I hope and pray he may keep! He brings a good character as a first-rate officer—from the

Sydney Dickens

last ship (this we have heard *not* from himself) which is so far hopeful!"

She was soon disillusioned. Although he now had a considerable sum of money from his father's estate at his disposal (his eventual bequest to his mother would amount to £6,000), she was outraged, as we have seen, when he refused to contribute to redeeming Dickens's little writing chalet from the Crystal Palace. And she was further outraged by the more serious matter of his refusal to help Dickens's favorite sister, Laetitia Austin, who was in severe want. "I feel so keenly that the omission of his only [surviving] sister's name in his will is the *one action* of his life which I *think unjust*—and unthoughtful on the part of my dearest Charles—especially as I know he had a great respect and regard for her—and that she was the one member of the family who had never asked anything of him, nor had any substantial help from him during his life. I can only account for the omission of any provision for her by his never taking into account that she should survive him."

Georgina changed her own will to leave Laetitia £250, but of course she was considerably the younger of the two women. She then organized the children, all of whom had funds on hand from their father's estate, to contribute £125 each to help ease their aunt's situation. All of them agreed at once—except Sydney, who indicated through his lawyers "that he was not disposed at present to place this sum in the hands of Mrs. Austin." "It *is* too disgusting," Georgina exploded. "I have no words to express what I think." At least she could change her own will yet again to remove her disgraced nephew from it.

Sydney would not live in disgrace for long. On May 27, 1872, just a few days short of two years since his father's death and having just turned twenty-five, Sydney died on board a hospital ship carrying him home on sick leave. One account says he died of bronchitis, another that it was an inherited heart condition. He was buried at sea, "with all the honours due to him, not only as an officer in the Service—but also as being the Son of one of the most distinguished men in England."

What can have caused Sydney's decline from being the lively, charming, good-natured Ocean Spectre to this sad spectacle of a demoralized young man? Georgina always believed that his deterioration was due to a severe fall he had undergone during his first cruise—that a brain concussion, followed by "African fever," had permanently affected him mentally and physically.

Predictably, she was relieved that Dickens had been spared the shock of his death (her first thoughts were always of Charles). To Annie she wrote, "Poor Sydney's *life* was his Father's most bitter trial and grief for several years before his death—and I fear we *must* feel that his being taken away early is the most merciful thing that could have happened to him, but it is very, very sad to have to feel this." A hard judgment, but Georgina was never a sentimentalist. "Well," she concluded, "he is gone, taken away, in his youth, from folly and *certain misery*, and is more mercifully and tolerantly judged now, than he could ever have been by his fellow creatures, and I am thankful that he is at rest. Peace be with him."

HENRY

IN CERTAIN RESPECTS, his father's death didn't change the way Henry, now twenty-one, was leading his life. He had several more years to spend at Cambridge, and his substantial inheritance ensured that he would face no financial difficulties in doing so. Home, however, was no longer Gad's Hill, which was now Charley's house. Instead, when Georgina and Mamie decided to set up house together, Harry joined them at 81 Gloucester Terrace, Hyde Park. He had his own considerable expenses at college, but as we have seen he insisted on paying for his room and board when he was with his aunt and sister on vacation. ("He won't come on any other terms," Georgina boasted to Ouvry.) Harry was always generous about money, but given his eventual responsibilities as the father of seven children, he could not always be as generous as he might have liked to be.

In 1872 he received his law degree from Cambridge, and in November of the following year he was called to the bar and took up his work with enthusiasm and vigor. "We have not seen him in his wig and gown, as he has not brought them home," Georgina reported, "but we mean to go one day to Westminster and see him in all his glory!" A year later, she could assure Annie Fields that he was "really getting on *capitally*, having done a great deal more than is usually the case with young Barristers," and later still she could report that he was "a bright good fellow," who always brought "life and spirits" into her tranquil home.

This pleasant living arrangement came to an end in 1876 when Henry married the French-Catholic Marie Thérèse Louise Roche, whose (Jewish) grandfather was the famous composer and virtuoso pianist Ignaz Moscheles. (The whole family was musical: Her mother had been taught by Chopin, and Gounod wrote a wedding march for Henry and Marie.) There were tensions over her religion—Dickens would have seen her Catholicism as "a terrible blow," Georgina announced—but the family as a whole liked Marie, who was good-natured, practical, prudent, and an excellent housekeeper and, very quickly, mother. Georgina to Annie: "We missed our dear bright *good* old fellow dreadfully at first. However such partings are in the natural order of things— very different from bereavements, thank God! and we are reconciled to the loss of Harry by the hope that he is going to be very happy in his marriage."

It was indeed an extraordinarily happy marriage, punctuated with the births of the seven children, beginning with Enid Marie the year after the wedding. ("Harry is very proud and delighted with his daughter—I need hardly say! It seems absurd to us that he should be a Father! He looks so very young, almost a boy still.") Soon there *was* a boy—Henry Charles Dickens. And then two more girls as well as three more boys, all of whose names would end with the obligatory "Charles Dickens."

Georgina Hogarth, c. 1905

In the Dickens tradition, Great-aunt Georgie, always close to Henry and his family, made up silly names for the children. Olive became "Olivey-Polivey." Elaine was Bobilow-Bobs. Hal, Halikins-Balikins. At times Georgina, especially as she grew older, would live with Henry and Marie, and her own homes were always near theirs. She was with them at the major holidays, and when they went on trips she usually went with them, helping to care for the children the way she had helped raise Henry and his brothers and sisters. It was a life of loving service, and she was loved in return. It was also a life of sharp observation and decided opinion. If she approved of Marie, we can be sure that Marie was worthy—"Dear Marie! . . . Who not only brings children into the world, but works for them in every way—incessantly after they come."

In *Recollections* Henry gives us a full account of his steady upward climb through his profession. It's obvious that he loved his work, and he describes with acuity and relish various cases he had been involved with, ranging from disputed grazing rights to murder, and furnishing his readers (many, presumably, in the profession) with affectionate yet astute sketches of his seniors and contemporaries, both lawyers and judges. He demonstrates a deep respect for the law itself and for the men of the law, showing a solid appreciation of his own merits as well as those of others. His practice grew as his experience did. He worked on the Home Circuit, centered in London, and then the Midlands Circuit, following the court with its judges around the country. His work also took him abroad, as when in 1907 he went to Jamaica for some months to represent the rights of an insurance company there.

A crucial moment in his career came when he decided it was time for him to "take silk"—that is, to apply to be approved as a Queen's Counsel, a risky step but essential if he was to move upward through the legal establishment. He was quickly accepted as a QC, and in 1912 was invited to go around the Midland Circuit as Commissioner of Assize, a step closer to his long-cherished desire to be named to the High Court Bench. It was not to be, through bad timing and ill luck, leaving him, as he says, with "a sense of bitter disappointment." But, he adds, "I do not want to be misunderstood. I am not at all putting myself forward as a man with a grievance. There may have been many reasons for my not having been appointed. It was a bit of hard luck—I put it no higher than that . . . After all, I feel I ought not to complain. I have had wonderful luck all through my life; more, indeed, than I deserve. I ought not to grumble therefore at one setback."

In 1917, a stroke of fortune: Henry was appointed the Common Serjeant of London, a central figure in administering the city's criminal courts, one of the High Officers of the Corporation of London, with (as he can't resist telling us) "all the powers and jurisdiction of a High Court Judge." This gratifying and satisfying job he held for fifteen years until he retired, writing to the Lord Mayor, "I do not think it fair to other men to keep on in this job indefinitely, as I shall be eighty-four next January. I could not, in the very nature of things, continue much longer, and I think it fair not unduly to delay my going. I think it is far better to go at the present time, when I know I am fully capable of doing my work on the Bench as well as I have ever done it, instead of lingering on with the feeling that I might be holding on to my post too long in the interests of justice." Sensibly, he dated his retirement as of October 1932, at which time he was to receive his full pension. Perhaps his greatest good fortune, apart from his marriage, was that he was a man who knew exactly what his path in life should be, and never deviated from it—three times, for instance, refusing the offer of a safe seat in Parliament. And he was well remunerated for his work. "I was fortunate enough as time went on, to gain a steady and considerable practice."

What kind of judge was he? We can see how he tempered formal justice with humanity by considering an account in

Henry Dickens

Recollections of a case of bigamy over which he was presiding. The laws at that time—as we know from the experience of William Thackeray—did not allow the dissolution of marriages in which one member of the couple was insane and permanently institutionalized. In this case, the father of four children whose mother was incurably insane found a good woman to help him raise his two little girls. As the girls grew older, it seemed important for their sake to regularize his domestic situation, and so he and the lady living in his house went through the form of marriage.

In passing sentence upon the prisoner I said this: "Prisoner at the Bar, you have broken the law; but you have done no injury to any mortal person on this earth. Your poor wife has long since been dead to the world; dead to you. Yet the law in its wisdom compels you to carry the burden of having this poor creature as a wife, so long as you and she remain alive. You are to continue to be bound in the law by those vows which have long since lost any meaning either for her or for you. You went through this form of marriage in order to make the lives

Caricature of Sir Henry Dickens by Spy

of your two girls easier and happier; and for no other reason. As a judge, I have to condemn you; as a man, I cannot bring myself to do so. You have my sympathy and I doubt not that of all kindly disposed people. You will be imprisoned for one day, which means that you will be at once discharged."

We can see how seriously he took the responsibilities of being a lawyer:

There are a few rules of conduct which should always be present to the mind of the advocate. They appear to be obvious; but what is obvious is not necessarily apparent to the human mind. Be courteous to your opponent and be polite but firm to your tribunal, whatever form that tribunal may take. Counsel is valueless unless he is courageous, and loses caste if he is rude. Never overstate your case in opening or you may have a fall. Your reply will come with crushing effect at a later stage. Take care not to "lead" your witness. It is not only a strict rule of law but absolutely imperative as a matter of expediency that his evidence should impress the tribunal as coming from himself and not as the mere prompting of his counsel. If there is a nasty fact which the other side knows of, open it yourself courageously and take the sting out of it. Be careful never to cross-examine a witness opposed to you as to his previous character unless you are certain of your facts; otherwise you may be doing him a grievous and irreparable injury . . . Above all, have the courage to be concise. This, in my opinion, is the most important rule of all, one which every tribunal—lawyers or laymen—would gladly welcome; and it is far more effective. A weary reiteration of the argument of counsel bores the jury and leads them to the conclusion that counsel does not believe in his own case. I have, as judge, often had occasion to pay a young man a compliment in court for his speech; but I have generally followed it up with a short note: "Capital speech, my boy; but far too long; far too long."

And we can see how his sense of humor enlivened and humanized his work:

On one occasion I was sentencing a very old hand—a "lag" of the worst kind—with all the dignity which the occasion required, when he interrupted me by saying, "You ain't a patch on your father." "I quite agree with you," I said. "What do you know about my father?" "Oh! I have read all his books." "Where?" I said, knowing that he had been in prison most of his life. "Well, I have read some in prison." "Have you?" I said; "that's capital; for you will now have eighteen months in which to resume your studies."

Wherever Henry went he was reminded of his father. When he was young and they were out together, Charles was inevitably recognized: One anecdote can stand for many. In Birmingham, visiting a big factory, "As we passed through the throngs of working men, I was constantly stopped by men reeking with sweat and grimy with dirt to ask me 'Is that Charles Dickens?' 'Is that Charles Dickens?'" Throughout his earlier years he was always seen as a son of the Great

Man and, he felt, unfavorably compared to him (as above)—an assessment with which he easily agreed.

Sometimes the circumstances were ridiculous, as when on a professional visit to the asylum at Broadmoor one of the lunatics approached him with "What! A son of Charles Dickens?" "Yes." "Take off your hat . . . Ah, a very small head. I am sorry to see a son of Charles Dickens with such a small head." Sometimes they were piquant and touching. In Jamaica, he tells us,

> I was taking one of my usual walks when I saw a buggy coming towards me with two chubby little black people—obviously a married couple—inside it. As they drew near I saw the woman nudge the little man as she recognized me, which she could easily do, as our portraits were spread all over the island, and when the buggy came abreast of me it stopped. "Mr. Dickens, sah!" "Yes," I said. "We are so pleased to meet you, sah! We know all your father's books. We have read them all and love them. We should think it a great honour to shake hands with you." This I did, and they went away with the brightest of smiles. This delightful kind of recognition by absolute strangers I had met with frequently before in different parts of the world; even in Moscow, where I was told that if the students of the university knew I was in town they would give a fête in my honour.

We can assume that being the son of his father had a positive influence on Henry's professional life, but as was true of his sister Kate as well, he grew into a figure in his own right, well known in London both for his accomplishments and for his genial presence. He was, he tells us at considerable length in his autobiography, a devoted theatergoer (as, of course, were his father and his oldest brother, Charley), and he moved in theatrical circles—Henry Irving was "a true and loyal friend." He was always devoted to music. (Lucinda Hawksley affectionately remarks that her favorite passage in *Recollections* is the sentence "I can only regard jazz as a passing phase in music, and not one that is likely to endure.") He knew many of the leading artists of the day, from Kate and Carlo's great friend Sir John Everett Millais to Sir John Tenniel.

He was an intrepid traveler, and he remained an ardent sportsman, especially engaged with anything to do with cricket and boating. A considerable section of his book is devoted to early boating expeditions in France, which he recounts with remarkable exactitude fifty years later, not forgetting to give practical advice to those of his readers who might want to follow him in this pursuit: "Take a liberal supply of boat-hooks, with extra sculls, tow-rope, wood, spare rowlocks, nails and necessary tools . . . Be prepared with two large pieces of waterproof sheeting to cover the luggage fore and aft. Do not forget guide-books, passports, maps and pocket-filters, and, above all, take as little luggage with you as possible." Sound counsel, as we would expect from this exceptionally sound man.

During World War I, he gave a series of readings of his father's work for the benefit of the Red Cross, and he and Kate joined together in a plea to the public to send copies of Dickens novels to men fighting overseas. He was active in founding a Boz Club (monthly dinners to celebrate his father) and, more important, the Dickens Fellowship—"to knit together in a common bond of friendship lovers of the great master of humour and pathos"—of which he was life president. The two main achievements of the Fellowship were the founding, in 1905, of *The Dickensian*, a monthly journal devoted to the publication of Dickens information and scholarship which is still active more than a century later, and the establishment of the Dickens Museum, at 48 Doughty Street, where the Dickens family had lived during the late 1830s. The Fellowship was instrumental in preserving the building from demolition in 1923 and re-creating the Dickens home so that we can stand in the room where the seventeen-year-old Mary died and see the desk at which Dickens wrote *Oliver Twist* and *Nicholas Nickleby*. Henry seems to have placed more importance on these various activities connecting him to his father than on the knighthood bestowed on him in 1922 for services to the Crown.

His sense of himself doesn't seem to have been affected by his very modest height. Hawksley tells us: "That Henry Fielding Dickens and his wife, Marie (known as 'Mumsey') were so diminutive has been recorded for posterity. In 1926 an amateur film was made of their golden wedding celebrations; in it their small stature is highlighted by the fact that their children, grandchildren and other relations all look like giants by comparison." Dickens himself was short, as were all his children, the tiniest, as we know, being poor Sydney. But Henry was also considered handsome, at least by his sister Kate. Writing to Plorn in 1874 she wants to know exactly how tall he is: "Mamie and I are still very small. I am afraid we don't grow with years, except in wisdom of course, H. is not

tall, but he is slight & nicely formed and is a very good looking young fellow I think and in his wig, is truly beautiful.
You will see the photograph, it is a lovely creature."

The relationships among the siblings were on the whole
placid and affectionate, except when financial disagreements
arose. When Mamie died, Henry turned over his share of
her estate to his sister-in-law Bessie, since Charley had also
just died, leaving her and her children almost without funds.
His relations with both Alfred and Plorn, however, eventually collapsed when they both not only failed to make good
on substantial loans he had made to them but failed to acknowledge his generosity or to offer explanations; this was
not only a matter of gratitude but a matter of justice. He was,
of course, always loving and attentive to his mother, extraordinarily close to Georgina, and usually on the best of terms
with Kate, although she and Marie didn't always see eye to
eye. All in all, he handled his position as the most successful
Dickens child with grace and tact.

Looking back over his long and productive life, we can
see that he possessed, and made the most of, the qualities his
father perhaps valued most highly: hard work, diligence,
energy. We can be gratified that Dickens died knowing that
at least this one of his worrisome children was on the right
path, and that, along with Alfred, he was worthy of his father's approbation. Knowing this was so must have helped
give Henry the healthy confidence that sustained him throughout his life: If he had pleased Dickens, he had nothing left
to prove.

Perhaps most important, he was blessed with a sound nature. Kate, in a despondent letter written to George Bernard

Shaw in 1898, had this to say: "Out of our large family of nine children, there was only *one* who seemed to me to be really quite sane. That was Henry, my lawyer brother, and I have wondered for years whether his sanity is to last through his life!" She needn't have worried.

Sir Henry and Lady Dickens, 1933

PLORN

WHEN HIS FATHER DIED, Plorn was still a minor, and did not come into his inheritance automatically. Georgina, as co-executor of Dickens's will, felt that "perhaps it would be dangerous to put him in possession of his income, before his age. Ouvry must realize how little boys were to be trusted with money—almost all of them." She suggested that he should have an allowance of £100 a year, but later when he was in financial difficulties—apparently he was working without salary on a sheep ranch—she was surprised that he hadn't asked for help. All the nephews, she wrote, were "generally so very ready to mention when they wanted money, that I thought his not applying for it was a sure sign that he did not want it." A year later, when he did apply, she replied that she and Forster, her co-executor, had determined that the amount of the allowance had been "carefully considered as being sufficient for his expenses in the Bush," and that if he really needed more, he had to produce a businesslike statement of his specific needs.

This reluctance of hers was certainly a reflection of the financial irresponsibility of most of the other nephews, but Plorn had always been unselfish and ungrasping about money:

Young Plorn in Australia

Remember, he was quick to offer funds to repurchase the chalet and to help his aunt when Dickens failed to include her in his will.

He was at this point in his life physically active and energetic—no one ever complained that he didn't work hard. In December 1872, he and two partners acquired a property of 300,000 acres on the Darling River, 180 miles north of the town of Wilcannia. Later, he was asked to manage the adjoining station of Mount Murchison, making him responsible for another 500,000 acres. Now a respectable citizen, he began participating in local affairs, serving as a justice of the peace, serving on the committee of the Church of England, and involving himself with the local hospital. But his chief interests lay in sporting activities. Various of his horses won important races, and he founded and captained a cricket team—"and a jolly good captain he was."

"Women," writes Mary Lazarus in *A Tale of Two Brothers*, "were seldom mentioned in the local paper and indeed there was a shortage of girls. According to the *Pastoral Times*, 'There is hardly a marriageable female in Wilcannia or within fifty miles thereof, and it is reported that a number of bachelors are about to leave the Darling for Sydney and Melbourne to try the matrimonial markets there.'" Plorn had even considered returning to England to find a bride, but in 1879 he met—and the following year, married—Constance Desailly, whose father had a station eight miles out of Wilcannia. Writing to Rusden of this happy turn of events, he assured the older man that "as we love each other very dearly, our future, will I feel sure, be a happy one." "We are going to take up our quarters at the old original head station, where there is a good, large, house, so we will have a very comfortable home. A home, that I, after roughing it for twelve years, will be able to appreciate." "It was right," Georgina wrote to Annie Fields, "that he should have a wife and home in the distant country where he had his occupation . . . God bless him dear old fellow! I hope and pray he may be very happy in his marriage."

His financial situation had improved: "As I am in the receipt of £300 a year will have no difficulty in supporting a wife." He also, in 1879, had come into an inheritance of £1,000 from Catherine. And then, Mount Murchison having been acquired by a much larger holding—"bigger than Ireland"—he either was fired or resigned and decided to leave Wilcannia. An auction was held to sell off his and Constance's possessions, but his departure from the town was delayed until January 1881, when the following appeared in the *Wilcannia Times*:

> We cannot allow the departure from among us of such a gentleman as Mr E. B. L. Dickens to pass unnoticed. Mr Dickens has been identified with the district for the last ten years, and has lately managed Mount Murchison station. During the whole of Mr Dickens's career he has always associated himself with true sport and conducted himself as an upright sportsman. Such a man is sure to make hosts of friends and his loss to a community like this is twofold, it deprives us of a through sportsman and the influence of a gentleman. We wish Mr Dickens success wherever his lot may be cast.

Plorn had made himself something of a figure in the area, as a station manager, sportsman, and citizen. And already stirring in him was an interest in politics beyond the local affairs of a small town in the outback.

It was now that Plorn and Alfred went into business together in Melbourne. But after an obscure commercial transaction under which Plorn acquired an area of desert land of between two and three thousand square miles—a transaction that led to a dead end—the brothers decided that he would return to Wilcannia while Alfred continued to run the Melbourne end of their business. However good a sportsman

Plorn may have been, it does not sound at this remove that he was an equally good businessman.

Re-establishing himself in Wilcannia was not a problem, and soon he was in the thick of local affairs. The town now had more than two thousand inhabitants and in good seasons was a prosperous center for the area as a junction of several roads and with steamers and barges plying the Darling. But there were fewer and fewer good seasons. The town continued to grow, but years of drought crippled life there and damaged the economy severely. Plorn may have been presi-

Plorn Dickens

dent of both the Cricket Club and the Jockey Club, but as an estate agent his business was adversely affected. Conditions worsened. In 1884 ninety steamers and more than one hundred barges "were stuck at different places on the River Darling." The heat was unbearable, the winds equally so; there was dust everywhere. The terrifying rabbit plague seemed uncontainable—the land was overrun. And the people of the area were feeling increasingly abandoned by the government of the territory. Their greatest need, they felt, was an extension of the railroad line from Sydney west to Wilcannia; as it was, their main—and unsatisfactory—connection to the world was south to Melbourne.

As his business faltered, Plorn's economic situation went from bad to worse. He was forced to beg a loan of £800 from Georgina, who couldn't afford it. Henry, somewhat reluctantly, came to the rescue and forwarded the money to Plorn, who neither acknowledged nor repaid it. The most likely explanation is that he used the money to shore up his business or to venture into new businesses, none of which succeeded, and was too mortified to explain or apologize. The breach between the two brothers was never adequately repaired. There is also the possibility that he lost the money gambling.

Through all this, however, Plorn, who had been elected an alderman, was involving himself further and further in politics, and in 1889 he was elected by a majority of two to one as the district's first representative to the lower assembly of New South Wales's parliament in Sydney. A newspaper derided him as having been elected only because he was his father's son, but he parried that humorously: "Sons of great men are not usually as great as their fathers. You cannot get two Charles Dickens in one generation," and when he added that he was proud of his name, he was cheered with cries of "Hear! Hear!"

Certainly he arrived in Sydney seriously determined to further the interests of his constituency. Again and again during the five years he served in the legislature he rose to speak of the desperation of his neighbors and of the need for crucial reforms.

People here [in Sydney] have no idea of the disadvantages under which these unfortunate men, the squatters of the western district, labour. To start with, they have a bad land law, and they are visited periodically by bad seasons. The proportion of good seasons to bad seasons is about one in four. Therefore if these unfortunate men do get their heads a little above water in one season they are dragged down again. I can assure hon. members that the position of these men is most deplorable and I consider it my bounden duty to make the House aware of the fact.

As a result of the lack of water, "in many cases the natural grasses, salt and cotton bush especially, are dying out and the rabbits in the western country have destroyed hundreds of thousands of acres of edible scrub that used to be the great stand by in the times of drought."

"He spoke strongly," writes Mary Lazarus, "in favour of compensating lease-holders for improving their properties, building and maintaining tanks and fences, for example. 'If the principle of compensation is adopted, improvements will go on to a very large extent and hundreds of men now walking about the country with swags on their backs will find work at reasonable wages.'"

Again and again he spoke of the disadvantages to towns like Wilcannia of being denied railroad connection to the capital of the colony, and of the advantages a railroad would bring: "If the railroad went to Wilcannia I feel confident that that town would become a big slaughter depot, as it appears now to be an acknowledged fact that it is possible to convey meat long distances in chilled cars."

His speeches reflect considerable personal knowledge of his district and of the problems confronting his fellow constituents, and his concerns reflect the reformist temperament displayed by his father in so many of his novels and articles— the father described and condemned the failures of society while the son tried to ameliorate them through political action. Alas, he made almost no progress and very little difference. The westerners lacked political heft, and his constant harping on their special problems left the legislature as a whole indifferent if not irritated. Throughout his five years of service, Plorn could feel only frustration.

Meanwhile, other problems were growing more serious. Angry, even violent, labor disputes; striking shearers and miners, bank panics, unemployment. Yet Plorn, always sympathetic to workers and their unions, stood back from these issues: "I always make it a matter of policy never to speak in Parliament unless I am familiar with the subject and can speak to some advantage." And the political tides had changed. In 1894 an invigorated Labour Party, led in his district by the new president of the Amalgamated Miners' Association, Richard Sleath, contested his seat aggressively. Sleath and his backers ran a ruthless campaign. For instance, in one of a series of highly charged and highly personal "Letters to Candidates" printed in *The Barrier Miner* and signed by "X," the writer wrote, "The most interesting thing about you is that you are the son of Charles Dickens. For of yourself you are not and never pretended to be brilliant; so that some folks have been led to exclaim, '*That* Charles Dickens's son!'" On the other hand, "X" began his "Letter to Sleath": "You are a born leader of men." The election was a rout. Plorn was defeated by a two-to-one majority, the very ratio of his victory years earlier. He never ran for public office again.

The year 1896 brought news from England of the almost simultaneous deaths of Charley and Mamie. Henry broke a long silence to convey the news—and to take up again the matter of the unpaid £800 loan, concluding "I have never been able to understand your inexplicable conduct to me and I never shall," immediately signing off as "Your affectionate brother." He also informed Plorn that in accordance with Mamie's will, he would be receiving a little less than £2,000, and hoped that £800 of that amount would be used to pay off the debt. This does not seem to have happened. At the same time, Georgina wrote of Mamie's death, and of distributing some of her personal effects. "Sad—sad work! . . . I hope Connie will like the necklace and ear rings we sent to her—in remembrance of dearest Mamie—with our love."

In a later letter, responding to one from Connie, Georgina writes, "I have not had a word either from Plorn or from you for more than eleven years! However now that our correspondence is renewed, I hope it will not drop again." She is concerned for Plorn's health, and concerned about the difficult times they are having. "I shall be very anxious for another report. Give him my dear love and with the same for yourself. Believe me always. Your very affectionate Auntie Georgina Hogarth." No further letters have survived.

Can Plorn's silence for so long a time stem from his mortification over the unpaid loan? Was there continuing resentment over the opportunities given to the four children who were allowed to live out their lives in England among the family? Perhaps anger that Henry had benefited unfairly by being sent to Cambridge? If these issues were ever acknowledged among the siblings, we have no record of it.

The £2,000 from Mamie must have been a lifesaver for Plorn and Connie. Their financial situation was dire, and Plorn was desperately searching for permanent remunerative occupation, concentrating on various possibilities in Western Australia, including the post of Secretary to the Department of Aborigines there. Among the people he applied to for recommendations was "my oldest friend in Australia," George Rusden, now seventy-nine. Rusden and others did what they could, but it was clear that such a job would have to go to someone from Western Australia itself. There was some buying and selling of shares, and Connie was earning some money as a professional typist, but she and Plorn were living on the edge.

In 1900, he did at last find work in the Moree Land District, as a purchase inspector. According to Lazarus, this work involved visiting properties purchased in accordance with the 1895 amended Land Act to make certain that the terms of occupation were being kept. "He was empowered to sue offenders who ringbarked trees or otherwise destroyed or removed timber on Crown lands or who allowed prickly pear to grow on Crown or private land."

Plorn was now living in the Criterion Hotel in Moree, about four hundred miles north of Sydney. Connie, no longer prepared to cope with his habitual gambling and drinking, was staying with her mother in Adelaide until, learning of his rapidly worsening health, she hurried to join him. Hearing of his illness, Kate and Henry had sent £100 "in the hope that it would bring some measure of comfort," but it came only after his death "of acute phthisis exhaustion" in January 1902. Before Connie arrived, the landlady of the Criterion helped take care of him—and he was behind in his rent. A young man, Rowland James Rudd, also living at the hotel, was kind to him as well, writing to his mother that he hoped to be sent some quail "for my friend Mr Dickens who has been on the sick list this last month." Rudd was with Plorn at the end. His will could not be probated since he died in debt, owing £172 10s 3d.

In Australia, not much attention was paid to his death. The Sydney *Bulletin* referred to him as "a decent, good tempered fellow," and there were modest mentions elsewhere. In London, the *Daily News* published a paragraph, ending "He was of a singularly amiable and winning disposition." As Lazarus points out, "amiable" was the very adjective used by his father to describe him half a lifetime earlier.

THE ELEVENTH CHILD

WHEN GLADYS STOREY'S *Dickens and Daughter* was published in 1939—to the outrage of Henry's widow, Marie, and other family members as well as other lovers of Dickens who felt that his reputation should be left unstained—it contained a throwaway line that ignited a controversy which remains unresolved today. Discussing the relationship between Dickens and Ellen Ternan, Storey refers in passing to "their resultant son (who died in infancy)."

What son? Born and died when and where? What evidence?

Storey doesn't make an issue of it—she never mentions it again—but her book is the direct result of her long and frequent conversations with Kate, who had asked her to write her biography. Storey's notes are preserved in the Dickens Museum, and Lucinda Hawksley tells us that "Having spent many hours painstakingly going through them, I was surprised how well documented her research was and how often Henry Dickens had backed up Kate's assertions." "Sir Henry and I . . . talked about Ellen Ternan—there was a boy but it died . . ." Unless you believe that Storey invented everything and left a trail of fake notes behind, you have to accept the fact that Kate and Henry were speaking the truth as they knew it. Indeed, why would Kate, who adored her father, invent such a story, and why would the equally adoring Henry have confirmed it?

There are also revealing letters from Dickens (in America) to Wills. According to Wills's nephew in 1934, these letters included instructions for dealing with "the welfare of a certain lady, then apparently sickening for her confinement. These instructions were of the most intimate nature and contained in letters which should have been destroyed at the time. Rudolph L. [Lehmann] and myself finally decided to send these half dozen letters to Sir Henry Dickens and that we did, and what became of them only his executors can now tell!" Claire Tomalin in *The Invisible Woman*, her book about Ternan, records a note made by Madeline House, a notable Dickens scholar who had spoken with Gladys Storey: "I'm convinced Mrs T [Ternan] was with Ellen at the time of the baby's birth. This I have from Gladys Storey, who—with Kate Perugini— read the letters from Dickens to Wills making plans concerning the baby, before destroying them,—It was something of a triumph to get this out of Gladys, who is a jealous guarder of her secrets; but I'm convinced by the way it was said and the way it came up that it was the truth G was telling me."

In *The Invisible Woman* Tomalin weighs the known facts and tilts toward the Storey account. In her recent biography of Dickens, she becomes a real detective, pursuing Dickens's complicated movements (and Ternan's) from London to rented houses outside the city and, more important, from England to France, to which Dickens made a series of short trips during the crucial time period. In 1863, for instance, "He was in France again in March for 'some rather anxious

Ellen Ternan, c. 1870

business' that detained him '4 or 5 days.' In April he wrote of a 'hasty summons to attend upon a sick friend' and a 'rush across the Channel.' . . . Then in August he wrote of 'evaporating for a fortnight' in Northern France, and again in November."

Tomalin refers to an American scholar, Robert Garnett, who surmised that the baby was born in January or February of that year and died in April; she accepts the birth date as plausible, but suggests that June is more likely as the month of the death, since it was then that Ellen was absent from her beloved sister Maria's wedding.

Two events frame this time period. In January, Dickens had attended a performance in Paris of Gounod's *Faust*, less than two years old at the time, and reported to several of his closest friends that this story of an innocent girl—seduced and betrayed by an older man, and who gives birth to an illegitimate child—had affected him deeply. "I could hardly bear the thing, it affected me so," he wrote to Georgina, "and sounded in my ears so like a mournful echo of things that lie in my heart." And to Macready, "I couldn't bear it, and gave in completely."

And in June he was in a train carriage carrying himself, Ellen, and her mother back to England, when there was a terrifying accident—people killed and maimed, and the three of them in a precarious situation until he effected their rescue (and went on to heroic efforts in rescuing or succoring other, less fortunate passengers). This was a sensational story, but he managed to have the names of the two Ternan women left out of it: It would have caused an uproar if it had emerged that he was traveling with them. This event, Tomalin underlines, was the first moment in three years at which Ellen can conclusively be placed. When at first they thought they might be killed, Ellen said, "Let us join hands and die friends"—a remark that suggests that things were not happy with them at this time. And how could they be if the baby had just died?

The evidence, as Tomalin lays it out, would seem to be conclusive even if circumstantial—there is no definitive document to prove things one way or another. (Which has not prevented other historians—Peter Ackroyd most forcefully—from asserting that the Dickens-Ternan relationship was never consummated.) Tomalin concludes her argument by stating that she is inclined "to believe the evidence of Dickens's

two children and Gladys Storey's notes, Dickens's own letters and the sequence of events described in this chapter—
that he was Nelly's lover, and that she bore him a child who
died. Even without documentary proof, and with uncertain-
ties remaining, the sum of evidence from many different
sources cannot easily be written off."

That is still a somewhat cautious conclusion. Seventy
pages later, however, in her account of Ellen's respectable
later life as wife and mother, she refers to Ellen's first legiti-
mate child, Geoffrey, as "the adored son who filled the place
of the son she had lost." Probability has slid into assumed
fact.

Persuaded by all this detective work and buttressed by
what seems to me common sense, I'm convinced that there
was indeed an eleventh child. We can only speculate over
what would have become of this boy if he had lived—how
Dickens, that master tactician, would have handled either
keeping him or hiding him. But we can be certain that both
he and Ellen suffered terribly through the ordeal of a concealed pregnancy, a secret birth, and a premature death. So
many of Dickens's fictional children die, and his own Dora
had died. Now the child he had with the woman he most
loved had died as well.

AFTERTHOUGHTS

THE GENERAL VIEW of the Dickens children is that, with the exception of Kate and Henry, they led failed lives. Dickens's own denigration of their characters and accomplishments has lent credence to that view: The boys in particular, as we have seen, were thought of by him—and talked about by him—as indolent, unfocused, even dull. His disappointment in them was not hidden from the world, or from them. He had the unshakeable belief, not uncommon in self-made men, that his sons lacked the rigor and discipline that he had displayed as he set out to make his way in the world.

But different young people take different routes to maturity, and the well-to-do children of one of the most famous men in the world could hardly be expected to confront life head-on in their mid-teens the way he had had to do to survive and prevail. We can regard the careers of at least several of the boys, and not just the well-adjusted, highly motivated Henry, as success stories, or potential success stories. Certainly Charley came into his own in his mid-thirties, both professionally and domestically, and lived a good and satisfying life. Sydney knew from the earliest age that he wanted the navy, and from all accounts he was extremely capable and well-liked until he foundered. Walter was doing well in the army in India until his demons—and his inherited physical vulnerability—got the better of him. Besides, how can we label a young man of twenty-two a failure? He had barely begun to live. Alfred, the older of the two Australian exiles, made a respectable effort, and having met with disasters outside his control, recovered and re-established himself while never losing his essentially optimistic and generous nature. Only poor Frank didn't really measure up; yet he doggedly pursued an arduous and unrewarding life of service.

The saddest story is that of Plorn, a sensitive and nervous boy who couldn't even handle a normal school situation and was then sent off alone, at sixteen, to the raw world of the Australian outback. What was Dickens thinking? This was his favorite son, yet in his unseemly haste to get the boys out of England—and financially independent of him—he in essence destroyed him. Surely, lacking his brothers' self-confidence and strength, Plorn could have been allowed to ripen a few years at home. But by this time Dickens was possessed by the near-madness that had torn his family apart, sparing no one, incapable of bearing criticism from others and with no capacity for self-criticism. After Catherine, Plorn was the family member most damaged by Dickens's mid-life rage and frustration. And Dickens, having committed this murder, could and did indulge in sentimentality and self-pity at parting from his beloved boy.

In addition to whatever deficiencies of temperament and character the boys (and, for that matter, Mamie) would reveal, and whatever unfortunate circumstances would confront them, most of them suffered as well from apparently inherited disorders. Mamie, Sydney, Frank, Plorn, and possibly Walter were undermined by drink. (Dickens liked to imply that Catherine was a drinker, but there's no evidence that she was. He himself was remarkably abstemious, though several of his siblings were not.) There was also a dangerous addiction to gambling in the Dickens family; even he acknowledged that this trait descended from his side of the marriage. Almost all the Dickenses were improvident and had poor business judgment, which is why Charles was so ambivalent about his own father, who like Mr. Micawber and Mr. Dorrit had been confined to debtors' prison, leading to the humiliations and hardships Dickens had endured as a young boy.

Finally, there were inherited physical weaknesses. Too many of the Dickens children died relatively young: Dora at eight months; Walter and Sydney (of heart problems) in their early twenties; Frank at forty-two; Plorn at fifty. Mamie and Kate were constantly ill, both as children and as adults; Charley, too, was constitutionally weak. Frank was almost deaf, and stuttered and sleepwalked.

How would the boys have fared if some way could have been found to keep them in England and give them time to develop at their own speed? Dickens clearly misjudged Charley, who once he was given a chance at a literary life did very well at it. It's hard not to conclude that, in the grip of the psychodrama involving his marriage and his passion for Ellen Ternan, Dickens wanted to have his life simplified by the dispersal of his children; the boys just got in the way. (The girls were excepted: He was always happy to have them with him. Girls presented no challenge—and no reminders of his own life. And he certainly honored and promoted Kate's artistic talent.) But well before Ellen he had the boys off at school by the time they were seven or younger, not to return home to their family for long months at a time.

And yet . . . what a wonderful father he was! He was at his best with little ones; once they approached adolescence he retreated. Without question the children loved their lives at home, undoubtedly reflecting his tremendous fondness for them and his unremitting interest in them. All their accounts of the fun and games, the warm focus he brought to their problems and achievements, his sheer *enjoyment* of them are convincing. They didn't even resent the discipline, the strict rules of neatness and punctuality. He was a magical father, he was a magical man, he was *Charles Dickens*.

As we have seen, five of the seven children who lived into their adulthood maintained a public connection to him. Mamie and Henry wrote memoirs of him; Mamie and Kate edited his letters, which Charley published; Charley, too, wrote of him, and he, Henry, and Alfred all gave public readings of his work. There was no way the connection could be forgotten or ignored—the Dickens name was so famous and beloved around the world that those who bore it could never really be anonymous. But it seems unlikely that they would have wanted to be. They may have been angered by his cavalier disposal of them and resentful of his easy domination over them, but not only were they fiercely proud of his accomplishments, they loved him.

DICKENS'S OTHER CHILDREN

A<small>ND WHAT</small> of all those other children to whom Dickens himself gave birth—the children with whom he populated his novels? Certainly, for no other important writer are children as central to the imagination as they are for Dickens. They dominate his early work. Immediately after *Pickwick* we get the orphaned Oliver Twist, the tragic Smike of *Nicholas Nickleby*, and the supremely pathetic Little Nell of *The Old Curiosity Shop*—the most famous child in nineteenth-century fiction . . . except for Alice in Wonderland. (Try to imagine two more different little girls.)

Dombey and Son gives us poor dying Paul and poor rejected Florence. The childhood years of David Copperfield and of *Great Expectations*'s Pip are the most powerful elements of their narratives. And of course there are many lesser yet vividly realized children in Dickens, from Oliver's partner-in-crime the "Artful Dodger" to the "Marchioness" in *The Old Curiosity Shop* to *Bleak House*'s harrowing Jo and pitifully neglected Jellyby children.

It's not until the final novels that the real-life children are old enough to serve as models for the fictional ones, although it's been suggested that the birth of Charley in 1837 may have spurred Dickens's thinking about childbirth in *Oliver Twist*, which he was writing at the time. (On the other hand, he himself, as the second-oldest child in a family of nine, certainly knew at first hand about the anxieties and fulfillments of childbirth.)

It has also been suggested that Mr. Gradgrind's wastrel son, Tom, in *Hard Times* may reflect aspects of Charley's character, but since Charley was only seventeen when that novel was published and had not yet earned (or deserved) his father's serious disapproval, I find that a dubious connection. Charley has also been proposed as a model for Herbert Pocket, Pip's good-natured friend in *Great Expectations*, and that seems a strong possibility; it's an affectionate portrait of a cheerful, buoyant young man. Peter Ackroyd, among others, has pointed out that when the novel was in the proof stage, Dickens struck out a reference to Pocket as being a prospective merchant in Chinese tea, and Ackroyd goes on to say, "He did not strike out a description of Herbert, however, which might be that of Dickens about his son. 'There was something wonderfully hopeful about his general air, and something that at the same time suggested to me that he would never be very successful or rich.'" That not only sounds like Charley but sounds like Dickens's idea of Charley.

Of the young women of the later novels, we can see in *Our Mutual Friend*'s Bella Wilfer not only elements of Kate Dickens—her brightness, her affectionate nature, her sauciness—but of the love between Kate and her father; Bella and Mr. Wilfer have that special bond that seems to have characterized the relationship between Dickens and his "favorite." There may also be aspects of Ellen Ternan in Bella—if Ellen was a little spoiled and a little flirtatious. (We hardly know her.)

These are slim pickings. There was, in fact, almost no overlap between the real children and the imagined ones. Indeed, it seems indisputable that the Olivers and the Nells and the Smikes are projections of Dickens's own unassuageable need to see himself as a fatally wounded child. *He* is the sufferer for whom all his tragic child victims are stand-ins. Imperiled Nell and tormented Smike and the homeless streetsweeper Jo and the dying Paul Dombey are not only powerful figures out of melodrama but vehicles through whom Dickens is expressing his rage and self-pity over what he saw as his harrowing childhood. Whereas Oliver and Florence and David Copperfield—David being the character with whom Dickens most closely identified—reflect the anti-masochistic side of his nature, the Dickens who rose above the persecutions of his childhood, actual or imagined, and triumphed over his persecutors . . . and the entire world. The fantasy of victimhood and the fantasy of vindication go hand in hand. Only toward the end of his life do these psychic imperatives recede and eventually evolve into the more psychologically mature narratives: *Little Dorrit*, *Great Expectations*, *Our Mutual Friend*.

"The children of his brain," Charley said, "were much more real to him at times than we were." Were his versions of his actual children—the feckless sons, the fond daughters—simply further inventions? To them he was compellingly real, but what were they to him?

A NOTE ON SOURCES

There is, of course, an immense Dickens bibliography, swollen recently by a burst of books celebrating his bicentenary. Even so, there are two absolutely essential texts: John Forster's biography and the twelve volumes of the letters (a marvel of editing).

Forster was Dickens's most intimate and trusted friend throughout his life, and was as well a judicious and practiced biographer. He was a faithful narrator, giving the world its first close (if occasionally cosmeticized) view of Dickens's life and nature—the first to reveal the story of the blacking factory, for instance, and the first to publish letters written by Dickens. But he was bound by the constraints of the day—Ellen Ternan has no place in his story—and by his responsibilities to the family, as well as by loyalty and affection. Nor was he one to hide his own light under a bushel—after all, he and Dickens were contemporaries and equals, unlike, say, Boswell and Dr. Johnson: a young acolyte and a man of commanding genius. Forster frequently overemphasizes his importance to the Dickens saga, but he was indeed central in his friend's life as well as to his work, and the entire Dickens literature is to a large extent dependant on his accomplishment: Everything starts with him.

The Pilgrim edition of *The Letters of Charles Dickens*, published by Oxford University Press, is a miracle of toil, tact, exactitude, and common sense. The three "General Editors"—Madeline House, Graham Storey, and Kathleen Tillotson—took thirty-seven years, from 1965 to 2002, to publish these twelve superb monuments of scholarship. It's also a prose masterpiece: Dickens's letters are astonishingly vibrant, fascinating, and fun.

Almost from the moment Dickens died, in 1870, the biographical mills began to grind. He was, after all, the most successful and beloved of all

English writers, whose popularity has never dimmed. Even before Forster, biographies were appearing, and over the next eighty years, others would appear, alongside personal memoirs of him and works of criticism and appreciation. Modern biography begins with Edgar Johnson's groundbreaking and popular two-volume work of 1952—a noble accomplishment, marred by its one-sided and unattractive view of the Dickens marriage. At least four other considerable biographies have since appeared: by Fred Kaplan (especially acute psychologically); Peter Ackroyd, whose grasp of history and literature is prodigious, and whose narrative is compelling and revelatory, even if he indulges himself in certain quirks of interpretation (his insistence that Dickens and Ternan never consummated their relationship); Michael Slater, a preeminent Dickens scholar, whose knowledge of Dickens's nonfiction output and accomplishments as an editor is unparalleled; and most recently, Claire Tomalin, who demonstrates commendable sympathy—and dogged investigative capacity. Tomalin is also the author of an outstanding life of Ellen Ternan, just as Slater is the author of a brilliant analysis of Dickens's relationship with women, which is the foundation of whatever understanding I possess of this crucial subject.

Books specifically centered on the Dickens children, and therefore central to my own work here, begin with Lucinda Dickens Hawksley's *Katey*, the biography of Kate Dickens Perugini, Dickens's favorite child and Hawksley's own great-great-grandaunt. Hawksley is an indefatigable researcher and a sympathetic interpreter, and she has a wonderfully appealing subject in her Aunt Katey. Almost as valuable to me has been *A Tale of Two Brothers*, Mary Lazarus's account of the lives of the two Dickens boys, Alfred and Plorn, who spent their adult lives in Australia. Her research is prodigious; there's no way I could have, on my own, traced the lives of these exiles in the outback, or for that matter in the other areas of Australia in which they lived during the latter decades of the nineteenth century.

Highly useful also was Arthur Adrian's *Georgina Hogarth and the Dickens Circle*, which not only gives us our fullest view of that central player in the Dickens drama but, due to Georgina's relentless correspondence, gives us countless insights into the lives and personalities of her nieces and nephews, whom she helped to raise.

Finally, and most recently, Lillian Nayder's *The Other Dickens* rights the balance on the subject of Catherine Dickens, convincingly demonstrating that Charles's rejected wife was a considerably more substantial and appealing person than he, with her sister Georgina's complicity, would have had us believe.

BIBLIOGRAPHY

The Pilgrim Edition of the Letters of Charles Dickens, volumes I–XII. Edited by
Kathleen Tillotson, Madeline House, Graham Storey, and others. New
York: Oxford University Press, 1965–2002.
The Dickensian. 1905–2011.

Ackroyd, Peter. *Dickens: Private Life and Public Passions.* London: Harper-
Collins, 1990.
———. *Dickens' London: An Imaginative Vision.* London: Trafalgar Square
Publishing, 1987.
Adrian, Arthur A. *Georgina Hogarth and the Dickens Circle.* New York:
Oxford University Press, 1957.
———. *Dickens and the Parent-Child Relationship.* Athens: Ohio University
Press, 1984.
Carter, David J. *Inspector F. J. Dickens of the North-West Mounted Police,
1884–1886: The "Christmas Carol" Baby.* Canada: Eagle Butte Press, 2003.
Dickens, Charles, Jr. *Dickens's Dictionary of London, 1879.* Charles Dickens,
"All the Year Round" office, 1879; reissued, London: Howard Baker, 1972.
———. *Reminiscences of My Father.* Supplement to the Christmas *Windsor
Magazine*, London, 1934.
Dickens, Sir Henry Fielding. *Memories of My Father.* London: Gollancz, 1928.
———. *The Recollections of Sir Henry Fielding Dickens, K. C.* Portsmouth,
NH: Heinemann, 1934.
Dickens, Mary (Mamie). *Charles Dickens by His Eldest Daughter.* London:
Cassell, 1885.
———. *My Father as I Recall Him.* New York: Dutton, 1896.
Dolby, George. *Charles Dickens as I Knew Him: The Story of the Reading Tours
in Great Britain and America, 1866–1870.* New York: Scribner's, 1912.

BIBLIOGRAPHY

Fields, James T. *Yesterdays with Authors*. Boston: Houghton Mifflin, 1887.

Fitzgerald, Percy. *Memories of Charles Dickens*. 1913.

Forster, John. *The Life of Charles Dickens*, 3 vols. London, 1872–74.

Hawksley, Lucinda. *Charles Dickens: Dickens' Bicentenary 1812–2012*. San Rafael, CA: Insight Editions, 2011.

———. *Katey: The Life and Loves of Dickens's Artist Daughter*. London: Transworld, 2006.

Hibbert, Christopher. *The Making of Charles Dickens*. New York: Harper & Row, 1967.

Johnson, Edgar. *Charles Dickens: His Tragedy and Triumph*. New York: Simon and Schuster, 1952.

Kaplan, Fred. *Dickens: A Biography*. New York: William Morrow, 1988.

Kitton, Frederic George. *Charles Dickens: His Life, Writings, and Personality*. New York: D. Appleton, 1908.

Kooiman, Dick. "The Short Career of Walter Dickens in India," *The Dickensian*, 2002.

Lazarus, Mary. *A Tale of Two Brothers: Charles Dickens's Sons in Australia*. Sydney, Australia: Angus and Robertson, 1973.

Lehmann, Nina and Frederick. *Familiar Letters: N.L. to F.L., 1864–1867*. Edinburgh: Ballantyne, Hanson, 1892.

Linton, Lynn. *My Literary Life*. London: Hodder and Stoughton, 1899.

Mathews, Charles James. *The Life of Charles James Mathews, Chiefly Autobiographical, with Selections from His Correspondence and Speeches*. Edited by Charles Dickens. London: Macmillan, 1879.

Nayder, Lillian. "Catherine Dickens and Her Colonial Sons," *Dickens Studies Annual*, 2006.

———. "'The Omission of His Only Sister's Name': Letitia and the Legacies of Charles Dickens," *Dickens Quarterly*, December 2011.

———. *The Other Dickens: A Life of Catherine Hogarth*. Ithaca, NY: Cornell University Press, 2011.

Rossi-Wilcox, Susan M. *Dinner for Dickens: The Culinary History of Mrs Charles Dickens's Menu Books*. Blackawton, England: Prospect Books, 2005.

Slater, Michael. *Charles Dickens*. New Haven, CT: Yale University Press, 2009.

———. *Dickens and Women*. London: J. M. Dent, 1983.

Storey, Gladys. *Dickens and Daughter*. London: F. Muller, 1939.

Tomalin, Claire. *Charles Dickens: A Life*. New York: The Penguin Press, 2011.

———. *The Invisible Woman: The Story of Nelly Ternan and Charles Dickens*. New York: Penguin, 1990.

ACKNOWLEDGMENTS

To Bob Cornfield, who has doggedly and acutely and sympathetically combed through the manuscript, and Adam Begley, always prepared (and equipped) to make me write more carefully.

To three Dickens authorities, Lucinda Hawksley, Lillian Nayder, and Michael Slater, who responded swiftly and generously to my requests for guidance, affording me the biographer's greatest pleasure: the opportunity for talking about his subject with other obsessed and knowledgeable parties.

To Robert Silvers for printing in *The New York Review of Books* my first public attempt to grasp Dickens. And to Marilyn Young for helping me penetrate and navigate the New York University library (which holds the complete run of *The Dickensian*, now well over a century old.) To Jennifer Kurdyla at Knopf, who has patiently dealt with a score of practical matters.

To all those at FSG who have worked in every possible way to support this effort, and to give me the book I wanted: Jeff Seroy, whose firm opinions on matters of editing and design are tactfully clothed in his habitual humor, kindness, and modesty; Jonathan Galassi; Greg Wazowicz; Sarah Scire; Abby Kagan, who so generously and good-humoredly let me share in the book's design; Charlotte Strick; Jesse Coleman; and my alter ego in things textual, Chris Peterson. This kind of work is pure fun when you're doing it with someone like Chris, who enjoys it and believes in it as much as you yourself do.

And to all the friends and acquaintances with whom I've been talking about Dickens for what seems my entire life, beginning with my wife, Maria, and including our daughter, Lizzie. Richard Howard and I were discussing him in college, and I can't possibly name all those who've come since, but they include Mary Blume, Carolyn Burke, Robert A. Caro, Diane Johnson, Julie Kavanagh, Alastair Macaulay, Janet Malcolm, Charles McGrath, Daniel Mendelsohn, Richard Overstreet, Claudia Roth Pierpont, Adam Sisman, Ileene Smith, and Brenda Wineapple.